An excellent read! Whether it's your first or fifteenth Ironman,
Nick Muxlow comprehensively delivers the key components to ensure a
very successful Ironman experience. *Journey to Kona* will not disappoint!'

Nancy Cullen MD FRACS, Multiple Ironman finisher, Hawaii Ironman Age
Group World Champion 2017

'A must read for any Ironman triathlete. Whether your goal is to
race in Kona, improve your performance, or complete your first Ironman,
Journey to Kona provides a fully comprehensive guide to training and race
preparation to ensure you can achieve your goals and enjoy the journey!'

Annette Eastwood PhD
Sports Physiologist
Honorary Adjunct Assistant Professor, Bond University
Former Senior Physiologist, Australian Institute of Sport/Triathlon Australia (2014-2017)
Physiologist with Australian Triathlon Team at Rio Olympic Games and three times ITU
World Championships (2014, 2015, 2016)
Former sports scientist at South Australian Sports Institute (2004-2014)
Ironman finisher

'A fantastic, easy to read book that covers everything you need
to know about finishing your best Ironman and, most importantly,
having fun along the way!
If you want to make it big you must approach your training
and your race with a champion's mindset and this book will guide you
in the right direction. I certainly wish I had access to this book
when I was a younger triathlete.'

Kevin Fergusson
2x Hawaii Ironman Age Group World Champion
5x Hawaii Ironman finisher
Over 30 Times Ironman Age Group Winner

'Training for and completing an Ironman is a significant personal challenge. Nick's book is an outstanding resource containing a wealth of science and experience-based advice and insight to help you prepare for, plan and execute a successful training plan and race. Highly recommended.'

Mary Mitchell
Ten-time Hawaii Ironman World Championship competitor
Multiple Age Group winner at Ironman and 70.3 distance races

'This book written by Nick Muxlow would have been invaluable to me when I first decided to tackle an Ironman event and compete in Kona. I started the journey with little knowledge of what lay ahead and what preparation was required. To have had Nick's book available to me at the time would have assisted me immeasurably in my preparation and training regime.'

Andrena Moore
Hawaii Ironman World Championship finisher
Age Group Winner, Port Macquarie Ironman
Age Group Winner, Ironman 70.3 World Championship Sunshine Coast Australia

'*Journey to Kona* is a comprehensive guide to all that you need to know and do to reach the pinnacle of Ironman. Hard work is not enough, you must train and race like a champion.'

Vincent Tremaine
Twenty-one time Ironman finisher
Ironman Age Group winner, New Zealand and Western Australia 2018
Four times Hawaii Ironman World Championship finisher

JOURNEY TO KONA

HOW TO FINISH YOUR BEST IRONMAN TRIATHLON, QUALIFY FOR HAWAII AND HAVE FUN DOING IT

NICK MUXLOW

Disclaimer
The material in this publication is of the nature of general comment only, and does not represent professional advice. It is not intended to provide specific guidance for particular circumstances and it should not be relied on as the basis for any decision to take action or not take action on any matter which it covers. Readers should obtain professional advice where appropriate, before making any such decision. To the maximum extent permitted by law, the author and publisher disclaim all responsibility and liability to any person, arising directly or indirectly from any person taking or not taking action based on the information in this publication.

To the West Lakes Triathlon Club – The Lakers – and any triathlete who has ever dared to dream of becoming an Ironman!

My wish is that this book inspires generations of Ironman triathletes, both at the club and the world over.

Believe in yourself!

CONTENTS

PART 1 – FITNESS FUNDAMENTALS

PART 2 – TRAINING TECHNIQUES

PART 3 – PERFECT PREPARATION

FOREWORD

When Nick Muxlow reached out to ask me to write a foreword for this book, I had to say yes. We're both from Adelaide and, although we belonged to rival clubs, the small, tight-knit community of triathletes in South Australia have nothing but respect for each other. After falling in love with triathlon and Ironman racing, Nick and I have both had success at an international level and have both competed in the ultimate race – Kona. The difference between us, however, is that I chose the life of the professional athlete, while Nick chose to become a professional coach. As a professional athlete I understand the importance of good, no-nonsense, comprehensive training. I also know how valuable a coach can be. Which is why I'm happy to recommend Nick's latest book.

Journey to Kona is a one-stop-shop for the aspiring Kona competitor. This book bundles all of Nick's expertise together and will help you with the all-important task of establishing a sound, no-nonsense training program – one that will enable you to not just complete Ironman races, but to truly compete. Nick's coaching is based on sound principles and good science. You'll find nothing crazy, whacky or outlandish, and no promise of a 'silver bullet' that will magically propel you across the finish line. Instead, you'll hear the message that has always resonated with me when it comes to Ironman training – that it's consistency and application that counts.

But *Journey to Kona* goes beyond simply providing a training program. Nick explains the 'why' behind the techniques and principles and the science that they're based on. Even on the professional circuit, I meet athletes who don't understand why they do what they do in training, and yet understanding these things can really help with motivation. Nick's book will answer the questions you have and help you understand why you should do what he asks you to do, making it so much easier to dive in the pool and hit the road. It's also a great reference book to keep handy as you travel further in your triathlon journey.

And, of course, the ultimate destination in that journey is Kona. Because Kona is the big one. It's got the history, the reputation, the crowds and the pressure. And the humidity, the heat and the pressure. And more pressure. Personally, I've found that having a coach has helped me do well at Kona. I don't know how I would set accountability goals and critique myself, let alone be a professional triathlete, without my coach Cameron Watt, so I feel that having a framework like the one offered in Nick's book is important for improvement. A coach is a second set of eyes that can analyse your training and provide a safe, useful and enjoyable training environment. As well as giving you important accountability, when a coach hands you a detailed training program it frees you up from the stress, planning and procrastination that can plague you when you choose to go it alone. All you have to do is check the day's set and head out the door. My life as a professional triathlete would be a disaster without a professional coach, but I understand that not everyone has that option. If you can't afford a coach, or just don't feel ready for that step, having a copy of *Journey to Kona* in your gym bag is the next best thing. It will make getting to Kona achievable and 'the big one' will become just another race.

Competing at Kona brings out the best in athletes, and if you can do well there you'll know you can cope with anything. When you stand on the start line at Kona, or at any triathlon or any big race, there are many factors beyond your control that might affect your result. There's nothing you can do about mechanical failures or the weather or other acts of nature, but you can do something about your preparation. If you leave no stone unturned in your training, you'll be in a great place when you stand on that start line. And that's what Nick's book will help you do – not just stand on the start line at Kona, but stand there feeling calm and confident and ready to celebrate the months of training that got you there.

I highly recommend *Journey to Kona* to anyone who wants to compete in the ultimate Ironman event. Happy training, and I'll see you on the start line.

Sarah Crowley, professional triathlete,
Kona competitor and Ironman athlete

- *3rd place, Ironman World Championship, Kona, USA*

- *1st place, Ironman European Championships, Frankfurt, Germany*

- *1st place, Ironman Asia Pacific Championships, Cairns, Australia*

- *1st place, Ironman South American Championships,*
  Mar Del Plata, Argentina

- *2nd place, Challenge Roth, Roth,*
  Germany (fastest Australian Iron distance)

- *1st place, ITU Long Course World Championships, Penticton,*
  Canada (Elite Women)

September 2019

PREFACE

Since writing my first book, *Journey to 100 – How to run your best 100km ultramarathon and love it,* why I coach and why I do what I do hasn't changed much; I simply have a bigger dream.

In short, I love to inspire people to achieve their impossible and reach their full human potential. But it goes deeper than that. Let me explain.

While many triathletes 'think' they can finish an Ironman and make it to Hawaii, they don't actually 'believe' that they can. Thinking that you can do something is all well and good; society is filled with people who 'think' lots of things but rarely take action.

Often when I start working with clients there is a glimmer of belief. This glimmer is just enough for them to take the first pivotal step and enlist the help of a triathlon coach. Sometimes their concern about their goal, their lack of belief and their lack of certainty that they can achieve what they hope to achieve is articulated when we first speak, while at other times it is only hinted at.

As a coach I believe in all my athletes. I often believe in them before they believe in themselves. For me this is a genuine feeling, and I believe that we are all capable of far more than we allow ourselves to believe. I also have the knowledge that my athletes don't yet have, and I'm aware that by outlining a path and taking clients through a process their self-belief builds. I nurture the athlete so that they grow and arrive at the start line full of confidence and certain that they can make the finish. I have seen it before and know that if they bring the right attitude and desire to the task, they too are capable of achieving their personal finish line.

Outlining a path and allowing someone to shift through that process from 'thinking' about completing an Ironman or indeed thinking about qualifying for Hawaii, to the beginnings of believing that they can – the point where they start to take action – is the first monumental tipping point. Previously I have inspired people through speaking with them individually, keynote speaking and being the best triathlete and coach that I can be. This time I decided to put it all into a book. To inspire many more people than I could ever hope to talk to in a lifetime. But also to unlock the power and self-belief that having a tried and tested path to follow can give you, the triathlete.

But there is also a deeper, personal reason why I wrote this book. This is the book that I wish I had access to as a younger triathlete. The book I looked for but couldn't find. I went about finding the information that follows in different ways. But that took years. I don't want you to miss out on Hawaii, like so many who want to get there but don't implement the right training and thus never realise their full potential and their dream. Instead I want to pull back a slingshot and catapult your knowledge and experience. I want you to enjoy training, I want you to train with purpose and I want you to utilise your training time to make the most improvement and most gains possible. I want to see you making not just fast, but rapid progress. But above all I want you to be treading water on the start line of the Hawaii Ironman.

Why I coach and why I wrote this book is bigger than an Ironman. More often than not, working towards an Ironman and qualifying for Hawaii goes hand in hand with personal growth. The Ironman is simply the catalyst. Sometimes this growth occurs during the training period, and at other times it follows the completion of the race. At first glance this appears counter-intuitive. But a journey to the finish line of Hawaii is more than just a triathlon race. It is an experience that shifts the triathlete way outside their comfort zone. It demonstrates to the athlete that they are capable. They now have an experience to prove that. Soon you will also have that proof and experience. Your Ironman and what follows in this book demonstrate what you can achieve if you put small meaningful steps together over a long period of time.

It teaches you dedication, it teaches you commitment, it teaches you to shoot for the stars!

You walk away believing that, 'If I can achieve this, I can achieve anything.'

So why do I coach and why did I write this book? To inspire, to educate, to help people grow, to allow them to achieve their Ironman goal and go on to achieve dreams they never thought possible. That is why I coach, that is the bigger picture of *Journey to Kona*.

Enjoy the adventure.

Embrace the challenge.

Always have fun!

Nick Muxlow
July 2019

INTRODUCTION

Emma ploughed along, checking her watch; 27km was the number she saw illuminated. The next aid station was about 2km ahead; she was deep in her race, but also deep in the hurt locker. The sun was setting, she was uncomfortably hot, her legs were shaky and the blisters on her feet were really starting to bother her. As the road started to climb she was brought to a walk. She ran the usual checklist over her body. Hydration: nope, that wasn't going too well, she was pretty certain she was dehydrated. Food: she hadn't been feeling good for hours and was struggling to eat. Her stomach felt woeful. She didn't even want to eat the favourite training foods she had with her! She simply didn't know what to do. Emma tried to break back into a run, but simply couldn't muster the energy. Exhausted, she stopped and sat, hunched on the grass to the edge of the footpath. One by one she watched the other runners continue on their way.

As the emotion of the event swept over her, she started sobbing. The course had eaten her up and spat her out, just like the bug you sometimes inhale accidentally when you're on the bike. 'Damn, this really isn't going well,' Emma thought. 'How can I qualify if this race just keeps beating me? All I want to do is qualify for Hawaii and I'm struggling to finish!' She thought back to the start line and asked herself, 'Why am I doing this? To prove to myself I can and to show my kids that if they set their mind to a challenge, they can achieve it.' With that gumption, Emma stood up and started walking again.

She could now see a cluster of glow sticks at the aid station ahead. She continued to walk, simply unable to run any more. When the volunteers saw her coming into the aid station on shaky legs, they offered her a chair that she took gratefully. Sitting down, Emma couldn't fight the fatigue and she started to shake, her eyes closed. The next voice she heard was a man's: 'Emma, Emma, I'm Dr Mc-Cartney. Emma, I'm sorry, but I am not going to be able to let you go on.' Too exhausted to argue, Emma knew that she wouldn't make the final 13km to the finish. The next thing she knew, she was on a camp stretcher in the makeshift hospital back at the finish line drifting in and out of consciousness. Dr McCartney mumbled about needing to put an IV drip in her arm. Lying there, the situation started to sink in. She had failed; she now had a DNF (did not finish) against her name.

Emma was devastated. Everything she had invested in that race had been wasted. Time, emotion, effort, money. And not just what she invested on race day, but also in the weeks and months leading in. All the time spent preparing in the final week before the race, as well as the time spent swimming endless laps in the pool, the hours upon hours on the bike and the countless training runs. The emotion of the event, and the emotional roller coaster she had put her family through as they supported her dream. The effort of organising the trip, and getting up early all those mornings to train before work. The money spent on the entry fee, the accommodation, the travel. The money spent on bikes, wetsuit, wheels, shoes, cycling shoes, pool entry, nutrition, cycling and running clothes and all the other little costs. And she was going to have to come back in twelve months to do it all again. Because she hadn't heard those magic words, 'Emma, you're going to Hawaii,' boom across the speakers as she crossed the finish line.

So what went wrong for Emma? For most Ironman triathletes it's normally not one big thing that goes wrong. Like a house of cards, the whole structure can come crashing down if just one element is slightly off and you don't have the know-how to tackle that challenge. The race can gradually wear you down, kilometre by kilometre. You can be left with a distance to the finish that would normally seem like an easy training run, but becomes an insurmountable hurdle, forcing you to withdraw from the race or, even more humiliating, be pulled out like Emma – so close and yet so far from the finish line, your dream and that magic little phrase, 'You are going to Hawaii.'

I'm sure you would like your story to be different. A story where you know how to tackle the challenges, where you have confidence at the start line, where you're prepared. A race where you get to experience the bliss of the final 100m to the finish line, feel the elation as your name is called across the speakers, create memories you never forget for all the *right* reasons and qualify for the elusive Ironman World Championships in Hawaii.

After competing and coaching athletes for over sixteen years, it has become apparent to me that without guidance, Ironman triathletes are going to make predictable mistakes. To prevent those mistakes, they need access to critical information as they proceed on their personal journey. While everyone's journey is different, the key lessons that triathletes need to move forward in their Ironman journey and their quest for Kona are inherently similar.

These are the same lessons that I personally had to learn as a young athlete when I entered the world of endurance events. I sought out mentors, clubs, coaches and groups to find this knowledge. At the time

I was blissfully unaware of the lessons I needed to learn and the order in which they would play out. It is only through hindsight, experience and coaching that I was able to recognise the consistencies in what, at first sight, appeared to be sporadic and disorganised progression.

Wouldn't it be great if the essential lessons, knowledge and understanding were laid out in one place to enable you to make not just fast, but rapid progress on reaching your personal Ironman goal? A book that set these lessons out in order, catapulting you from one valuable lesson to the next, and collectively giving you the fundamentals and experience required to become a successful Ironman triathlete and the best chance to qualify for the Ironman World Championships in Hawaii.

This is where *Journey to Kona* steps in. We're going to take you on a journey, a journey to the finish line of your best Ironman triathlon. That journey starts today. We are going to start from where your current knowledge and skill set is at, and build on that to deliver you an incredible Ironman education that will give you tremendous confidence. Confidence that you're doing the right training, confidence that you're prepared for the challenges ahead, and confidence that you will make it to the finish and have pride in sharing the amazing story of your best Ironman and hear not only those famous words, 'You are an Ironman!', but also hear the elusive sentence that follows, 'You are going to Hawaii.'

A good plan ensures the fundamentals are in place early. This allows you to enjoy your training. You finish races, you set PBs[1], and you're

---

1   Personal Bests, also known as Personal Records

motivated because the challenges you face are part of racing and you have a skill set that allows you to work through them. Sure it's not always easy, and you don't always get it right. After all, this isn't your local 5km fun run, this is 226km (140.6 miles) across three disciplines: swim, bike and run. You didn't sign up because it was going to be easy. You signed up for a challenge, to push your comfort zones to find out what you are truly capable of.

WHY LISTEN TO ME?

As well as over sixteen years competing in and coaching endurance sports, I also have a degree in Human Movement and Education. That means I understand sports, especially triathlon, and I understand the education and learning process. This is different from many other coaches, who don't come from a background of education. For me, a large part of coaching is educating the athlete. I understand that learning comes through doing, through guidance, through making mistakes, through creating experiences.

But I'm not just a coach; I'm also a competitor. It all started long ago when I had a boyhood dream of completing the Hawaii Ironman. It's a dream I achieved, but it took hard work and commitment, and required me to develop a deep understanding about long-distance triathlon racing – Ironman racing. This goal challenged me, it pushed my comfort zones and it forced me to find out what I was truly capable of.

Highlights for me as a competitor include competing at an age-group level in the World Sprint Distance Championships on the Gold Coast in Queensland. I competed in Budapest the following year, also on the Australian Age Group team, except this time I competed over the standard-distance triathlon race (1500m/40km/10km). In this race I clocked my standard-distance PB of 1.53.09. My initial start in short course triathlon racing set me up well to expand into Ironman triathlon racing. Following these events the fascination and allure of Ironman racing gripped me as I pursued my childhood dream. In total I completed seven Ironman races with a PB of 9 hours 10 minutes. Of course, one of these was the Ironman World Championships in Kona, Hawaii.

WHO ARE YOU AND WHO IS THIS BOOK FOR?

We know that you want to finish your best Ironman, and perhaps you have previously tried to finish one without success. You might have had a DNF or DNS (did not start). Maybe you didn't have a great first experience, but are now more open to learning and looking for information about how to finish an Ironman with confidence. To sum up, this book is for you if:

- You're an experienced triathlete, having completed many sprint- and standard-distance races. Maybe you have even completed one or two Half Ironman 70.3 events. (If you haven't completed many events, don't worry; you will just receive a super fast-tracked Ironman education!)

- You have not completed a Half Ironman 70.3 triathlon, but wish to as part of your build up towards your Ironman event.

- You want to get out of your comfort zone. Awesome! This is a big step and you're now looking for some guidance.

- You can see there is so much information out there, but you're not sure what applies to you as an Ironman triathlete.

- You have completed an Ironman but it did not go as well as you would have liked. In fact, it was a flop!

- You have completed a solid Ironman but didn't qualify, and you are still on your quest for Kona and looking to pick up on some 1%ers – the missing piece of the puzzle to help you get there.

- Your sights are set on completing your best Ironman, but you have triathlon ambitions beyond completing just one event and you want to qualify for the Ironman World Championships in Hawaii.

- Triathlon isn't just an event, it's a lifestyle you love.

If you are yet to complete an Ironman the first step is gaining this experience, and this book will guide you along your way. You may qualify for Hawaii the first time. If so, this is fantastic – but rare! If not, don't be disheartened; you need to repeat the process. Grow and improve as an Ironman triathlete, front up at the start line again, and don't give up. I know people who qualified first time, but I didn't qualify until my fifth attempt, others don't qualify until their tenth attempt, and then there others who ultimately get there through a legacy spot.

THE UNIQUENESS OF TRIATHLON

Triathlon is complex; it is one event made up of three different disciplines. This presents a unique challenge that is often misunderstood. You are not a swimmer, you are not a bike rider and you are not a runner. You are a triathlete and as such you need to train like a triathlete – in this case an Ironman triathlete.

Over any given training week you will train in each discipline. This creates a unique interplay between training sets. This interplay must be taken into consideration when constructing a training plan. This is why it is vitally important that if you look to a coach for a training plan that you do not go to a swim, bike or run coach – you must go to a triathlon coach.

Other peculiarities which occur in Ironman triathlon are the need to run a marathon 42.2km (26.2 mile) after you've got off a whopping 180km (112 mile) bike ride. This sensation is one that can only be understood after it has been tried. Transitions are another unique element to triathlons, and knowing how to prepare and navigate these is unique to triathlon and multisport racing. While transitions are short compared to the entirety of the event, if you want to qualify for Hawaii you are going to have to nail these. Many a slot to Kona has been decided within the transition compound!

Lastly, you must be aware that you are not a pool swimmer. You are an open water swimmer. Championship pool swimming occurs in a highly controlled environment where the maximum distance swum is normally 1500m. They do this with the sole aim to swim as fast as they can for this distance and be completely exhausted by the time they make their final touch on the wall. This is very different from swimming 3.8km in open water. The triathlon swim occurs in a highly *un*controlled environment; swimmers are everywhere, often on top of you. There is current, waves, chop, sighting, and this is only the first part of the race. You need to have an efficient stroke for the demands of triathlon because, at the conclusion of the swim, you are going to have to get up, ride 180km and then punch out a marathon. You are an Ironman triathlete.

Within the uniqueness of triathlon we must also understand that each triathlete is unique and each course is unique. While the distance remains the same, some courses are flat and others hilly. Each of these complexities will influence the demands on your body in different ways. Added to this, the way each person responds to these factors is entirely unique, due to each person's strengths and weaknesses when it comes to each discipline. It is not uncommon for a triathlete to be stronger in one of the three legs. This is certainly okay, but it adds an extra complexity when looking at a training program.

While this may initially appear confusing, you have to accept that triathlon is a unique sport – that's the nature of what you are tackling.

IRONMAN EXPLAINED

I also need to mention here that throughout this book, and indeed in the title, we use the term 'Ironman'. In this case we are simply referring to the distance of the triathlon event: a 3.8km swim (2.4 mile), 180km (112 mile) bike ride and 42.2km run (26.2 mile).[2] Ironman is simply one of many brands that offer triathlons of this distance. I certainly don't mind if you complete an 'Ironman' branded race, 'Challenge' branded race or one of many other smaller brands offering a triathlon of this distance. The knowledge is of course transferable to any triathlon of that distance. However, for simplicity, throughout this book we will always refer to Ironman because to qualify for Kona you will have to do so at an Ironman branded race.

---

2   To keep things easy from now on we will simply refer to the distances using the metric system, so simply substitute the number you are used to working with.

SO WHERE SHOULD YOU START?

Planning is not sexy, in fact for many it's not even fun when all you want to do is swim, bike and run! But an Ironman is not a leisurely half marathon, a century cycling race, or even a 70.3 event. This is a full IRONMAN! The difference between a single-discipline event and a 70.3 event is huge. From here the jump from a Half Ironman to a full Ironman is exponential, as you are effectively starting the race again without recovery!

I'm from the land 'Down Under', where Ironman Cairns is our Asia-Pacific Championships. The number of competitors who sign up and don't finish are extraordinary. In 2018 that number was a touch over 17%, with many not even making the start line! Between the time they laid down their cold hard cash for the entry fee and race day, they have had to abort their dream. Injury may have struck, their 'why' may not have been strong enough and many simply didn't have the gumption or know-how to get through the event, despite managing to get to the start line. But you are not only aiming just to get to the start line, or even the finish line, you are aiming to qualify for Kona, and to do this you need to be in the top few per cent of finishers; you need to be at the pointy end of the field.

If you're going to complete an Ironman, you need a plan. And if you are going to qualify for Kona you need an exceptional plan. This plan is about increasing and developing your knowledge, under-standing and implementing long-distance training principles, and getting you to that final 100m of red carpet bliss before the finish line. This is where you know you are going to finish. Where you soak it all in and everything becomes worth it. Where you cross the finish line, hear those magic words 'You are an Ironman' and accept the little reward – an Ironman finisher's medal. If you have put in the work and raced your best Ironman you will get the added benefit of securing a ticket to the Big Island – to compete in the Ironman World Championships in Hawaii. Your quest for Kona will be complete.

The benefits you will receive by following our methods are many:

- You will be confident at the start that you will make it to the finish line and have a great race.

- You will have focus and a purpose for each training set you tackle.

- You will give yourself the best chance to finish and avoid the dreaded DNF, or worse, DNS.

- You will develop into a strong Ironman athlete.

- You will have a specific plan of action.

- Your motivation will skyrocket.

- You will give yourself an Ironman education, and understand how the many concepts and different elements of long-distance triathlon apply to you.

- You will be confident that you are investing your training time well, and giving yourself the best training adaptations.

- You will have more fun training.

- You will achieve your goal and have a catalyst for life outside your triathlon. You'll think, 'If I can achieve this, what else can I achieve in my life?'

- All going well you will qualify for Kona!

WHAT TO EXPECT FROM THIS BOOK

I will start by making sure that you understand fitness, both mental and physical; you will know *why* you have to do what you do in training. From there we will go on to discuss training in more detail, and ensure you know exactly what is required of you when it comes time to swim, bike and run. I will finish by showing you how this all comes together in the Ironman training plan, culminating in your Ironman race day. In the appendices, you'll find a super-detailed training program designed to suit someone working a standard Monday to Friday, nine to five job, plus the guide you need for interpreting and adapting it. This plan will be based around a 24-week (six month) build into your goal Ironman. You will also find a substitute plan which can be used should you wish to complete a 70.3 event in your lead-up to your Ironman event. If you are currently yet to complete a 70.3 event we highly recommend completing one as you progress on your journey to your full Ironman.

Throughout the book you'll find the heading **YOUR JOURNEY** popping up here and there. This is an invitation for you to take action; sometimes you'll do this with a pen or pencil, and at other times you'll need to head out the door to swim, bike and run. I can guide you and provide you with the information required to become a successful Ironman athlete, but you also have to take action to improve your Ironman knowledge and experience. You need to implement the lessons discussed to develop the understanding and, most importantly, the experience necessary for you to become a successful Ironman finisher.

BECOMING THE TEACHER

As you read the book we recommend two things. Firstly, grab a highlighter and highlight important points as you go. Secondly, share your thoughts and discuss the concepts with others when out training. Being able to teach another about these concepts gives you a much deeper understanding than if you only read them. You may find yourself having to refer back to the pages to consolidate your understanding. The net result is that when you hit the start line, your knowledge base will be much higher than the person on the right, who has not read the book, and the person to your left, who only read the book but never discussed the concepts or taught the concepts to others. Become the inquisitive student and become the teacher.

I will also mention here that if you have read my first book, *Journey to 100*, you will find that many of the concepts discussed in here have been covered in that book. While running 100km and completing an Ironman triathlon are vastly different endeavours, the training principles behind both are underpinned by the training principles of all endurance events. This book could not be produced without including much of the material already covered in that book. This time we are looking at these training principles through the lens of finishing your best Ironman triathlon. Hence, while the concepts are the same, the lens is so vastly different that I am certain you will find great value and insight in reading on.

If you have read that book and already feel confident in the concepts discussed, feel free to skip these parts – you'll figure out where they are – and simply read the new parts that are relevant to Ironman triathlon. However, I certainly do recommend some light revision, as on subsequent reads you often gain more clarity and a deeper understanding of the content.

So, if you're ready, tighten your goggles, grease your chain, don your shoes and read on. You are about to embark upon the best triathlon of your life!

PART 1

FITNESS FUNDAMENTALS

At the start of your journey, you're motivated. You head out the door and train to your heart's content. But then you might find that you start to fall behind in your training – when the demands of that thing called life get in the way. And as life continues to pile on, your initial enthusiasm might start to fade, and you begin to wonder how you will ever make it to a finish line that looks so distant.

Or you might have been training consistently, then suddenly, three or four weeks in, bang! That sore knee turns into ITB[3]. You're back further than square one! At this point you would need to commence a rehabilitation program,

3   Illiotibilal band friction syndrome

then a return to training program. That dream of your best Ironman, let alone qualifying for Hawaii, is out the window – at least for the time being. If only you had understood your body better and taken the right precautions to prevent injury, that race date would still be locked in.

Yet another Ironman athlete might jump straight ahead to the Ironman training plan, start training well and make great progress, but feel their overall fitness simply isn't improving. It turns out that while their fitness across all three disciplines has made steady progress and they're in amazing shape, they haven't understood the Ironman nutrition essentials. Imagine how much further their fitness would have improved had they been open to this particular lesson earlier.

This first part of the book is all about getting some basic understanding in place before you start building towards your dream Ironman. This way, you'll avoid a lot of the common mistakes that both new and seasoned Ironman triathletes make.

CHAPTER 1

MENTAL FITNESS

I bet when you saw the title of Part 1 that you thought it was all going to be about your body. And in fact most of it is. But one of the most crucial elements of training for – and completing – your best Ironman triathlon is ensuring that you're mentally fit and that you have the right mindset. The training and planning that you will undertake on your journey to your best Ironman will go a long way towards giving you confidence, but there are some other factors at play here. So first and foremost, let's make sure your head is in the right space. This is all about mindset, motivation and making sure you're jumping on this journey for the right reasons.

MINDSET

Mindset is your mind's ability to train and race. The first thing you need to bring to the table is a can-do attitude. In triathlon, this positive mindset includes your attitude towards training *and* racing. Do you have long-term consistency in your training? Do you have the discipline to train? Even when it's wet, cold, humid or hot? Or do you make excuses? Are you mentally tough when it comes to the back end of a training set or race? What's your resilience like when the going gets tough? You certainly didn't get into this because it was going to be easy! Are you able to achieve a state of flow (being fully immersed in the present moment) in training and racing? Can you endure peak sensation (the uncomfortable feeling you get when racing hard)? What is your mindset on the start line? Do you believe in yourself and your abilities?

At a basic level, a positive mindset is necessary from the start. What you may not have previously recognised, however, is that this is likely to be a strength of yours. If you were not mentally strong, I doubt that you would even be considering completing an Ironman or backing up for a subsequent Ironman. Come race day a positive attitude, along with a bit of grunt, is important, but we can't overlook the need to develop your ability to both endure peak sensation and utilise flow.

MOTIVATION

In Australia we have a hot Christmas and New Year; it's a great time to be outside running and being active. But every year my training partners and I witness the same phenomenon. In the first week of January there are people running and cycling everywhere because those New Year's resolutions are strong. But by the second week of January numbers are already dwindling, and by the third and fourth week things are back to normal. What happened? What went wrong? All these people with great intentions simply didn't stick to them. All because their 'why' wasn't strong enough!

So now I'd like to ask you a question.

WHY DO YOU WANT TO FINISH AN IRONMAN?
AND ASSUMING THAT YOUR WHY IS BIGGER THAN THIS,
WHY DO YOU WANT TO QUALIFY FOR HAWAII?

This is a question you're likely to be asked frequently. Friends, family and work colleagues will all ask this question. Not being among the converted, they may struggle to understand your mindset. Here are some of the answers to the question 'Why finish an Ironman?' that we often hear at The Kona Journey:

- To get outside my comfort zone.

- To experience something incredible.

- Because I always push my limits, why would triathlon be any different?

- To undertake a life-changing experience.

- To achieve something I never thought possible.

- For the amazing journey.

- To reach the finish line and hear the words 'You are an Ironman.'

- For the lifestyle and the community; because I love being fit and socialising with friends.

- I love the freedom – it regularly lets me escape the daily grind.

- It's my catalyst for life – if I can do this, I can do anything.

- It adds the structure I need to my life; without structured training I'm lazy.

- To finish a triathlon was my midlife crisis, and now I love it.

- I want to qualify for Kona.

And these are the common answers we receive to the question 'Why do you want to qualify for Kona?'

- To qualify is to push myself further than I ever have before.

- I want to experience the magic that is the Ironman World Championships.

- I want to run down Ali'i Drive and feel the buzz.

- I want to challenge myself against the best in the world.

- I want to experience the biggest one-day endurance race in the world.

One, many or all of these reasons may apply to you. Whatever the reason or reasons, you must ensure that *you* understand *your* reason(s) – why *you* are doing it. This is important because, at some point in your training, you will need to draw on that motivation. It's generally in the middle of training, when the first flush of enthusiasm for your goal has passed, but you're too far from the end to see your goal and the finish line. You're caught in the middle of the journey, and you're tired, fatigued, hungry and grumpy, and wondering if it's really worth it. This is when your 'why' needs to be strong, so that you can draw upon it. You certainly don't want to drop out!

YOUR JOURNEY

Know your why. Why you are choosing to finish an Ironman? And why do you want to qualify for Kona? What are your big five reasons for doing this? List them. The big five! If you don't have five, that's no problem, but the first one or two have to be really strong reasons for why you are choosing to swim, bike and run 226km. You don't want weak reasons, such as:

- It sounds like a good idea.

- My friend said I should.

- I won a bike.

You want inspiring reasons. So, using the earlier list as your inspiration, I want you to list your big five:

1.

2.

3.

4.

5.

With your whys now established, what do you do with them? As discussed above, at this stage you're likely to have oodles of motivation. It's down the track that you're going to need to remind yourself of your whys and access the emotional energy they contain. To ensure that your whys form a regular part of your training plan, you need to periodically remind yourself of them. Rather than create arduous and time-sucking tasks, let's find simple ways to do this. My favourite is to write your five whys on a piece of paper and place it under your car's sun shade. This way, when you're driving and stuck in traffic, you can take out your five whys and remind yourself of why you embarked upon this extraordinary, life-changing experience.

The other tip I have is to put them into your electronic calendar, whether that's on your phone or another device, as an event on the first day of each month. This way, they'll pop up as a reminder every four weeks – just about the time that they start to drift from your conscious thought. This will help to keep you focused on the task at hand.

Okay then, time now for you to hop to it and take a couple of minutes to embed your whys into your long-term training plan. Do it now, and when you receive your monthly reminder, you'll have a pleasant surprise and be glad you took the time to get properly organised.

HABIT

Motivation is important, without a doubt, but there are some tips and tricks that we can all employ to help support that intrinsic desire. The number one lesson that you need to take from this book is that to be a successful Ironman triathlete you must have long-term consistency. If this is not in place, then you simply won't progress beyond 'GO'. To create long-term consistency, a triathlete must ensure that two important factors are present. The first is that your training must be a priority.

Everyone is busy, but we all get twenty-four hours in a day. A good triathlete will put their daily training sets at the top of their to-do list. They will be done before other less meaningful tasks. The cleaning can wait, the washing can wait. They will make sure it happens. They will get up early, they will train after the kids have gone to bed. Rain, hail, shine, typhoon, they will find a way to swim, bike and run. The point here is that training has to become one of the top priorities for your day. When it does, you will feel better for it.

The second important factor is that your training must become a habit. Good triathletes build positive training habits into their daily life and schedule, and the best way to change a 'bad' habit is to replace it with another habit – a 'good' habit. In the triathlete's case, no training is replaced by training. When you start your Ironman journey your motivation will be high, which will help you create your new habit. It takes approximately three weeks to build a habit, so if you've made training a priority, it won't be long before it becomes a habit. After the three-week point, training every day becomes much easier. It's your new habit.

With the habit established, you don't have to think about it much, and you can conserve a lot of your mental energy. Things will start to become automatic and you won't have to work so hard to find your motivation, which can start to decline in the middle stages of your journey.

PLEASURE AND PAIN

At this point, it seems fitting to discuss the two critical forces that shape your life: pleasure and pain. Author Anthony Robbins discusses these in depth in his book *Awaken the Giant Within*.[4] These two forces will influence every decision that you make in life, so it's important that you shift your understanding of the power of these two forces from your subconscious to your conscious mind. This is particularly relevant when it comes to triathlon training.

You have to learn to attribute great pleasure to training and great pain to not training. And while you can utilise both pleasure and

4   Anthony Robbins, *Awaken the Giant Within – Take immediate control of your mental, emotional, physical and financial destiny*, Free Press, 1992

pain to your advantage, we prefer to focus on the pleasurable things in life and draw on these. At any time when you're in the heart of your training program and you're considering wagging your planned set, you need to consciously think about the decision you're making. Why is it that you want to skip a set? For example, are you attributing greater pleasure to having coffee with friends than completing your set? This will lead you to think your training can wait, but you're likely to find it doesn't get done. You may need to shift a waning mindset. In this instance you need to shift your focus from the small, short-term pleasure to the enormous, long-term joy of finishing your Ironman and getting to Hawaii. After your Ironman is over – and the Ironman World Championships are over – then you can have coffee to your heart's content and share your amazing story. And it only takes an instant to change your focus and ensure your swimming, biking or running takes top priority.

On the flip side, maybe you're attributing great pain to going out and training in the cold; after all, your bed is nice and warm and cosy, and another hour of sleep wouldn't go astray. You can change this mindset in an instant by focusing on how great you will feel when you get back and the endorphins that will be running wild around your body.

To help in your quest to maintain your motivation and utilise these two forces, you need to turn the intensity up. You need to intensify the feelings associated with your choices. This is where emotion steps in. These two forces can't simply be given lip service; you have to feel them in the depths of your heart. You have to feel that pain with such emotional intensity that you take action; only action will rectify a potential poor choice. In each of the above examples, and in the constant barrage of choices you face on a daily basis with regard to your training, the thought of training needs to become pure emotional ecstasy.

When you bring the forces of pleasure and pain into your conscious mind and create a high level of emotional intensity around them, you can utilise them to help you stick to your plan and achieve your dream.

EMBRACING CHANGE

Now that we've talked about boosting motivation and confidence, let's consider something else you're likely to be looking for from this Ironman experience: to get outside your comfort zone. Outside your comfort zone is where growth occurs. Growing as a triathlete and utilising the lessons learnt training helps to create positive change through your entire life. You have two options here: you can be a reluctant learner or you can embrace learning. To embrace learning means you embrace positive change. Yes, that's a scary thought for many! So scary that I'm going to say it again: embrace positive change.

To have learnt something means that you have progressed, you have created new neurological pathways – you have changed. You understand new concepts, you understand things at a higher, better or deeper level. Yet people are reluctant to change. Given you have picked this book up and, most importantly, started to read it, I'm going to make an assumption – you're among the minority who like rapid progress and development and you embrace fast change.

Problems will sometimes arise, but only because you have not been exposed to the concepts or knowledge required to continue on your journey – you make decisions based on the best knowledge that you have. Two things need to happen. First, you need to be exposed to new knowledge. That's why you're reading this book, go you! Second, you have to be open to taking this knowledge on board; this is known as a growth mindset. So don't be afraid to grow and change.

Given that you want to get out of your comfort zone, grow and are open to positive change, I want to finish this chapter with a challenge. I want to help you discover some areas of triathlon that you may not be aware of or may not have been exposed to before. To help fast-track this process the business that I founded as a way to inspire triathletes to complete their best Ironman and reach Kona, The Kona Journey, has developed a quiz that covers the essential requirements to be an Ironman triathlete, all of which, of course, are revealed in this book.

The Triathletes Quiz consists of twenty questions that determine the extent to which you are likely to succeed as a long-distance triathlete. This quiz gives you a personal triathlete score. Along with a score, you're also provided with a personalised Triathlete Report that is emailed to you. This personalised report will discuss your strengths and focus areas, as well as give you specific actionable points and training sets that you can utilise immediately to improve your ability as a long-distance triathlete. I am super proud of The Triathlete's Quiz and the benefits that it provides to you, the Ironman triathlete.

YOUR JOURNEY

To whet your appetite, prime your mind for what is coming and have a bunch of fun, jump online and take The Triathlete Quiz now. You'll find it here: QUIZ.THEKONAJOURNEY.COM

The quiz can be accessed on both mobile devices and desktops, so there's no excuse. It works best and provides the most benefit if you take it before reading on. It's great to get a starting point of where your current knowledge is at before I start your Ironman education. You can take the quiz as many times as you like. This allows you to later determine your improvement. You may take the quiz again after finishing the book, or at any stage you wish to see how your Ironman triathlon knowledge has progressed. Keep in mind, however, that knowing and understanding is one thing. Implementing the knowledge, lessons and experience into your own triathlon training and racing takes continual commitment to your personal triathlon improvement. This is going to require you to swim, bike, run, tackle challenges and improve your triathlon experience bank. As you can appreciate, there is a lot to look forward to in the coming pages.

◦◦ ◦◦ ◦◦ ◦◦

Knowing your why, making training a habit by ensuring it's a top priority, embracing change and linking strong emotional pleasure to what you're doing will go a long way towards giving you confidence for your Ironman journey as you progress towards Kona. It's also important that you know where you're at with your knowledge, and are willing to learn and fill in any blanks you have. But probably the most important boost to your confidence – your positive mindset – will come through following a structured program. It is through meeting the challenges of a specific Ironman training program and through tackling the Ironman journey that personal growth occurs. The end result is increased belief in yourself and your abilities. You hit that start line with confidence. So read on to learn and grow as an Ironman triathlete.

CHAPTER 2

PHYSICAL FITNESS

We now shift our attention from the psychological to the physiological understanding needed to become a successful Ironman triathlete. I'll warn you – there's a lot of science in this section! But if you want to finish your best Ironman and reach the Holy Grail, you need to understand what's going on in that magnificent machine of yours – your body!

FITT – WHAT IT MEANS

To complete an Ironman, you need to be fit. Really fit. And the best way to improve your triathlon physiology – your fitness – is to use the principles of progressive overload. Gradually overloading the body causes it to respond to the stress that you place upon it, which in turns causes it to adapt and become stronger. Continual repetition of this process delivers what you see as an improvement in fitness. An improvement in fitness means that you can swim, bike or run between points A and B quicker, or with less perceived effort.

But all this begs the question: what is fitness? You probably know that the word 'fit' was originally an acronym that stood for 'Frequency, Intensity and Time'. These three factors, with the addition of a second 't' that stands for 'type', form the basis of your training program – FITT. Let's now look at each of the letters in the acronym in a little more depth, in particular how each principle relates to triathlon.

FREQUENCY

This is the measure of how frequently you train. If you train with greater frequency, this increases the load you're placing on your body. For instance, if you swim, bike or run for forty-five minutes twice a week, and then increase this to three times a week, you will increase the load you place on your body. Your body will respond with an increase in fitness.

INTENSITY

Intensity is the measure of how hard you're training. Going out for an easy swim, bike or run is great and you will certainly make improvements early on by doing this. But if you start to vary the intensity at which you train, you can fast-track these fitness gains. Exactly how hard and how long these intensity efforts last can be based upon a range of factors, including age, training history, injuries and goal race, to name a few. These factors and the way they interact as part of your overall Ironman training plan are highly individualised.

The main concept that you need to understand now is that increased intensity places increased demands on your body. Your body responds to the increased load created by an increased intensity with an increase in fitness. For example, if you were to swim, bike or run for one hour and include ten blocks of hard training for one minute, you will get to the end of the training set with a higher level of fatigue (in basic terms, you would be more puffed out) than if you had simply completed the set at an easier pace for the entire hour. This is despite each set taking the same time to complete. Hence the intensity that you train at, along with the frequency at which you train, collectively determines the load you are placing upon your body.

TIME

Time is the last element that can affect your overall load. If you swim, bike or run for forty-five minutes, you place a forty-five minute load on your body. If you train at the same pace for sixty minutes, you're placing a greater load on your body. You are asking your body to 'work' for longer – in this case fifteen minutes longer.

As triathletes we don't often consider how long we train for; the measurement that we prefer to use is kilometres or miles. However, when we look at things from a coaching and training perspective, what you're really looking at is how *long* you trained for – the number of minutes or hours, not kilometres or miles. This is especially important when hills are involved. On a flat road, the distance you cover in, say, one hour, could be vastly different from the distance you cover on a hilly training set in the same time frame. Does this mean that your hilly bike or run placed less 'load' on your body? Probably not, and this is because the overall time spent 'working' was likely to be higher in the set that included hills. As cycling routes in particular regularly feature hills and sometimes mountains, we need to take this into account. You need to be able to reference the distance completed against the time spent training. To give you a concrete example, if you normally cover 30km per hour when cycling, then hit the hills and only cover 24km per hour, don't be concerned. You will have still placed a similar load on your body; one hour of exercise is one hour of exercise.

TYPE

Type refers to the type of exercise you're doing. Triathletes are lucky in this area because three disciplines make up the event. This means that you are spoilt for choice. While there is certainly some cross over and interplay between the disciplines, it is important to understand that to become a better swimmer you need to be swimming, to become a better cyclist you need to be cycling and to become a better runner you need to be running. There is some grey area here, however. Other endurance activities, for instance cross-country skiing or kayaking, as well as playing team sports (the more running involved the better), can improve your fitness. But the benefit obtained from these is largely dependent on how fit you are. As you increase in competence and fitness, you will find these other activities benefit your triathlon to a diminishing extent. Unless you are new to triathlon you will have passed the point where other sports will benefit you, so it's going to be best to stick with swimming, biking and running where possible.

TRIATHLON FITNESS

So, now that we've reviewed exactly what fitness is, let's make sure we understand four areas we need to develop in order to improve your body for Ironman triathlon. These are your aerobic capacity, muscular endurance, lactate threshold and economy.

AEROBIC CAPACITY is your body's ability to use oxygen to deliver energy. This is the area that most people start developing first, which is great. It's also one of the most important components required for triathlon and developing it can be very time consuming. However, it is only one part of the complete picture.

MUSCULAR ENDURANCE, sometimes known as **STRENGTH ENDURANCE**, is the ability to maintain a high-force output for a long period of time. This is crucial to being a successful Ironman triathlete. The two key parts to this are 'force' and 'time'. The force needed when completing a triathlon is the ability to push back on the water, exert force onto the pedals or push down on the ground when running, all of which consequently push you forward in the respective disciplines. This occurs whenever you train. Endurance refers to the ability to do this over a prolonged period. Combining the two gives us the following: you can push back on the water, exert a force onto the pedals or push down on the ground with a high force for a long period of time. An understanding of this concept and how to train it is one of the key parts of becoming a successful Ironman triathlete. Muscular endurance ensures that you have strong arms and strong legs over the back part of each discipline. Developing this ability is often one of the most overlooked aspects of Ironman triathlon. Understanding and developing this area is a key determining factor between those who complete their Ironman successfully and those who complete their best Ironman and qualify for Kona.

LACTATE THRESHOLD is the point at which your muscles start producing lactic acid quicker than it can be removed. The key point you need to learn here is that if you can increase your lactate threshold, you can sustain a solid pace for longer. You are faster, your fitness has improved. In short, improved lactate threshold equals improved fitness.

This is generally one of the areas where experienced athletes stand to make the largest fitness gains. Beginner or novice athletes don't need to focus as much of their training on this area, as generally they still have plenty of improvement to make in terms of aerobic development. Later in the book we'll discuss how to determine your lactate threshold in each discipline and how to improve it.

The last of the physiological elements that you want to improve as a triathlete is **economy**. Economy is the oxygen cost required to swim, bike or run at a particular speed or pace. Often confused with efficiency, efficiency is 'the ratio between the mechanical energy produced during exercise and the energy cost of the exercise'.[5] While similar, these are not the same. As an athlete it is easiest to understand the key concept in terms of how efficiently you're able to swim, bike or run. In other words, the amount of energy required that allows you to travel at any given pace. The longer the triathlon, the more important efficiency becomes. This is because, as the distance of the event increases or, more importantly, as the time taken to complete the event increases, you are working at lower and lower speeds. This means you need a good return on the energy invested. Given your goal of an Ironman, ideally I want you to be very efficient in each discipline; I want you to be an efficient triathlete.

Unfortunately, improving your economy can be challenging. While economy fits under the physiological elements, the way in which you are most likely to improve your economy is by improving your technique. We'll look at technique in more detail later, but for now let's explore the two energy systems for the Ironman triathlete.

5   http://run-fit.com/wp-content/uploads/runningeconomy.pdf
     Accessed 3 July 2019

AEROBIC AND ANAEROBIC ENERGY SYSTEMS FOR THE TRIATHLETE

As a triathlete your focus is on improving your aerobic threshold and your anaerobic threshold. You need to improve your aerobic threshold so that, at increased paces, you are still working aerobically instead of tipping over into the anaerobic zone. Improving your anaerobic threshold allows your body to better tolerate or clear lactic acid, which means that you are able to travel faster when you enter the anaerobic zone. While you do not race above or near your anaerobic threshold for an Ironman, improving it has the net result of helping to drag up your aerobic threshold, which you definitely want to do. Improvement in either of these areas constitutes an improvement in fitness: you are fitter. Consequently, if you improve both of these you will see greater results than if you focused on only improving one. However, while you're improving the body's energy systems, remember that this is separate to swim, bike or run strength, which is discussed in Chapter 7.

At this point you also need to have an understanding of coupling and decoupling.[6] Your heart rate and pace are said to have remained consistent, or 'coupled', if they have not risen or fallen in relation to each other between the start and finish of a steady aerobic training set. This concept holds true for each of the disciplines; however, it is best illustrated through an example. If you go out for a steady aerobic run of, say, two hours, at the start of the run your pace would correlate to a particular heart rate. As the run continues, fatigue will start

6   Joe Friel, *Total Heart Rate Training – Customise and Maximise Your Workout Using a Heart Rate Monitor*, Ulysses Press, 2006

to develop. If, at the end of the run, your heart rate has increased while your pace has stayed the same, your heart rate is said to have 'decoupled' from your pace. What this means is that to achieve the same pace you have to work harder – run with a higher heart rate. Decoupling can also occur if you maintain the same heart rate but your pace drops off.

As an Ironman triathlete, first and foremost you need to build a large enough aerobic engine to power you through the entirety of your race. Developing this aerobic engine is one of the main focus points of the long swim, bike and run discussed later. Once your aerobic engine is developed so that decoupling does not occur, then you are able to move on to developing your anaerobic engine. This does not mean that one is ever completely neglected in the Ironman training program – it is simply that these form the different focus points. Your goal is to first develop your aerobic engine so that decoupling does not occur, and then you can look to fully develop your anaerobic engine.

＊＊＊＊

Ka-pow! Now you have an understanding of exactly what fitness is and the principles of progressive overload that lead to an improvement in fitness. Further, you understand the most important areas of fitness that an Ironman athlete needs to develop as well as the two areas often overlooked by athletes wanting to complete their best Ironman. In the next chapter we'll look in depth at the most important letter in the FITT acronym – intensity. More importantly, we'll learn how to measure it.

CHAPTER 3

THE 'I' IN FITT

Intensity – the 'i' in the word fit – is probably the most important aspect of fitness. But, frustratingly, it can be the most difficult to understand and measure. In this chapter, we're going to deepen your understanding of the markers that measure intensity, and introduce you to a simple, but effective way of identifying and measuring it.

Intensity is how hard you're exerting yourself when training, specifically the physiological response that your body is undertaking to deliver the required effort. Every athlete, from the fastest to the slowest, has a range of speeds from rest through to max. When training at various speeds and effort levels, the body will respond in different ways and produce key physiological responses. It is important that you understand what these are and when they occur with reference to your personal training.

As a triathlete it is also imperative that you understand that this is different for each discipline. That is, in each discipline you have a range from rest through to max. The key determining factor, threshold heart rate, which is discussed in length shortly, is different for each discipline. The reason why this occurs is because of the different recruitment of muscles in each discipline. In the swim you are supported by water and are predominantly using the smaller arm and back muscles to propel you through the water. On the bike you are again supported, this time by the seat. However, on the bike you are now predominantly using the larger leg muscles as you ride. Finally, on the run, you have to support your entire body and you are using your large leg muscles to propel you. Collectively this means that your threshold heart rate varies. It will be lowest for the swim, in the middle for the bike, and the run will be the highest of the three.

This is important for triathletes. You need an awareness of training intensity in order to follow a detailed training plan. Not having this understanding can lead to two problems. The first is under-training, where you're not working hard enough, which means that the time spent training is not as well invested as it could be. The second is training too hard, which also means that your training time is not well invested and, worse still, this can lead to the extreme of over-training, which unfortunately is not uncommon in Ironman triathletes. Further, if this understanding is not developed through the training program, come race day you risk going out at an unsustainable pace and will be left walking to the finish line or worse still, you guessed it, the dreaded DNF. Understanding intensity is essential so that you can learn about pacing across each discipline, then go on to create a pacing plan for your training and racing. We'll learn more about this in Part 2.

KEY TECHNICAL TERMS

To develop our complete understanding of intensity, we need to develop our understanding around the language used in this area: aerobic vs. anaerobic exercise, VO2 Max, heart rate, breathing, rate of perceived exertion (RPE) and, finally, our beloved power. You need to be familiar with all of these terms so you can use the training zones table introduced later in this chapter, which will be key to your training.

AEROBIC THRESHOLD

This is a key marker in the body at which lactate levels start to rise just above resting levels. When working aerobically your body is primarily using oxygen to burn carbohydrate and fat to deliver energy. We'll understand this more when we look at nutrition later.

ANAEROBIC THRESHOLD

This is the other important marker in the body. It's another term for the lactate threshold introduced in the previous chapter that is a key development area for Ironman triathletes. This is the point at which lactic acid accumulates in the working muscles quicker than it can be cleared away. The best way to understand this comes from a useful analogy provided by Dr Joe Friel, who likens it to pouring water into a cup with a hole in the bottom. Normally the water just flows straight through. If, however, you increase the amount of water you're pouring into the cup, it gets to a point at which it can't drain out the bottom as fast as you're pouring it in. In other words, it starts to accumulate. This is the equivalent of your lactate threshold.

VO2 MAX

Also known as aerobic capacity (don't get this term confused with aerobic threshold; they are very, very different), VO2 Max is the maximum amount of oxygen an athlete can use from their blood in a minute. However, for this number to be reached the athlete is also well in excess of their anaerobic threshold. This measure used to be considered the Holy Grail of endurance performance. However, as the understanding around endurance sports has increased, this measure has become largely irrelevant. Anaerobic threshold has a much greater effect on determining your performance because a higher anaerobic threshold will help to simultaneously drag up your aerobic threshold. Improving these two key markers, aerobic threshold and anaerobic threshold, will have the greatest effect on your Ironman triathlon.

HEART RATE

Heart rate is an important consideration for triathletes, and the improvement in heart rate monitors means they're popular and a fantastic way to track and help you understand your various intensity levels. However, this type of tracking comes with a very real risk: over-reliance. People become overly concerned with what their heart rate monitor is telling them. They start to micro-manage themselves through technology, and forget to listen to their body and what it's telling them.

The heart rate monitor does provide a great benefit for the triathlete, however, and we recommend using it in training. The heart rate monitor should be used to help develop an understanding of intensity levels by cross-referencing your heart rate with your RPE and your power meter (if you have one), all of which we'll discuss shortly. Once this awareness has been developed, the triathlete becomes a more proficient triathlete, as they no longer need the guidance of their watch. Their understanding is now internal. While not needed once this point has been reached, triathletes should continue to wear their heart rate monitor for the advantage it provides from a training analysis perspective.

In order to develop this intrinsic understanding, it can be helpful to complete training sets where you cover up your heart rate or change the displays on the watch so that you simply can't look at what your heart rate is doing. Once you've completed your set, you can then review it to see how you went, relative to your training outcomes and focus. If you still can't resist the temptation to take a peek, simply leave the strap (and even watch) at home and just enjoy your training set!

You need to be aware that heart rate is variable, and can be affected by a number of outside factors. Fatigue levels, heat, cold, humidity and hydration – all of these can affect your perceived effort level relative to your heart rate. You need to be aware of the impact that these factors have, especially if you're referencing heart rate to pace or speed, because you could have a great set but feel that you are unfit, not training well and heading backwards when this couldn't be further from the truth.

BREATHING RATE

Your breathing rate is one of the most underutilised methods for determining intensity. Once you have paid conscious attention to your breathing rate relative to your RPE and heart rate, it can be a very accurate way to help you determine your output. For those of you who are competitive – and chances are that you are – you can even use this as a guide for how your competitors are going!

In a race (or even in training), every time you pass or are passed by another cyclist or runner, listen to their breathing. You will soon develop an understanding about how hard they're working. This can be very comforting when you get passed during a race; you will often be able to tell if you will be seeing that competitor again later in the race, or if they are indeed a superb triathlete who is likely to finish in front of you.

RATE OF PERCEIVED EXERTION – RPE

Before power meters, before heart rate monitors and before GPS devices, there was rate of perceived exertion (RPE). RPE is a scale used to determine the effort that you *feel* you are performing at. RPE is based on a scale from 0–20, where 20 is an all-out max effort.[7]

For the Ironman triathlete, having an intrinsic understanding of RPE is incredibly important. A highly developed understanding of this and how it applies to you is the ultimate goal. When training, all the other methods of determining your exertion levels (heart rate, pace, power, etc.) are simply a guide to help you develop your sense of RPE, or reassure yourself that what you *think* you are doing – how hard or easy you are training – is in fact what you *are* doing. With practice you will become very good at simply knowing your output, and when you do, you will have taken a huge step forward in your ability as an Ironman triathlete.

The big benefit you will find with using RPE is that it takes into consideration how you are feeling that day. Easy, steady, moderate hard, hard and very hard are all relative to you. With this method, over time, you become aware of your own personal capabilities.

The other benefit is that you automatically take into consideration the time interval you're being asked to complete. For instance: if you were to complete ten minutes of very hard training and one minute of very hard training, you will push yourself very hard for both. Your pace or speed would be different for the two, but you will take the difference in time into account and naturally select what is 'very hard' for you.

7   In some literature RPE may be expressed as a value between 0-10 to further
     simplify things.

POWER

When on the bike, and increasingly on the run, you have an additional marker to measure your intensity: power. This has been made possible by the invention of the power meter, and over recent years power meters have gained popularity as their cost has dramatically decreased. The reason that power is so useful as a measurement is that it takes into account many of the variables that affect your speed when cycling or pace when running. When cycling, heart rate is a good measure of your intensity, but speed is not. Speed is affected by wind, drafting (only in training, of course!), hills and road surface, to name some of the big ones. This means that your speed becomes a poor measure of your intensity. Power takes all these into account and looks at the effort you are putting out. Likewise, for running, hills, headwinds and other variables are all taken into account when we use power as a measure. What this means is that this measure is independent of your heart rate, and power simply becomes another way to measure your intensity. However, it must be used in harmony with other measurements and take into consideration heart rate and RPE.

While power meters are still expensive, if you have the funds available they make an exceptional training tool for the bike and run. But I will say it now: you absolutely do not *need* a power meter to finish your best Ironman or to follow the training plans discussed later. From now on I will include the term power where relevant; however, if you are not using power as a measurement, then you will simply use heart rate or RPE instead.

YOUR JOURNEY

Here's a great little set to try that will enable you to develop an understanding around your RPE. This set is best completed on the bike or run.

WARM-UP

10 minutes easy

10 minutes steady

MAIN SET

5 minutes steady

4 minutes moderate hard

3 minutes hard

2 minutes very hard

1 minute walk or spin

Repeat the main set three times.

COOL DOWN

10 minutes easy to cool down

The aim of the above set is to ensure that there is an increase in exertion as well as pace or speed/power over each segment.

MEASURING INTENSITY – TRAINING ZONES

It's now time to introduce you to a table that you will need to look at frequently as you embark upon the training sets discussed later in this book. It's an intensity zones table.

The purpose of this table is to give us a common language to use when discussing your effort levels: how hard, fast or intensely you are training. The table allows us to discuss your effort at different levels (zones) from rest through to max. You may have seen various tables like this, but I recommend that you choose one and stick to it. And given that this whole book is based on this particular table, I'm not really giving you much choice in the matter. Rest assured, however, that this table has been chosen because it's simple and easy to use for the Ironman triathlete – you.

A word of warning: as a triathlete you have the added complexity of needing to understand your zones across each of the disciplines. As you work out your target heart rates, power zones, or swim pace (discussed at depth in the next chapter), you will need to establish these for each discipline.

INTENSITY ZONES TABLE – SWIM, BIKE AND RUN

Zone	Effort	RPE (rate of perceived exertion)	% of LTHR (lactate threshold heart rate)	% of maximum heart rate	Zone information and descriptors
1	Active recovery	10–12 Easy	<84%	<71%	• Recovery • Easy swimming, cycling, jogging • Start of warm-up pace • Easy pace between intervals • For Ironman finish time over 12 hours you will operate in this zone
2	Aerobic	12–14 Steady	85–91%	72–76%	• Aerobic training • All-day swimming, biking or running pace • Concentration required to maintain effort • Controlled calm efficiency • Breathing more regular than at Zone 1: when running often 4 steps to inhale and 3 steps to exhale • Fatigue sensation is low; however, after this zone has been held for many hours it can become hard due to the accumulating fatigue • Swimming, riding or running pace often used on the 'easy' part of a Fartlek set • For Ironman finish times between 8-12 hours you will operate in this zone

Zone	Effort	RPE (rate of perceived exertion)	% of LTHR (lactate threshold heart rate)	% of maximum heart rate	Zone information and descriptors
3	Tempo	14–16 Moderate hard	92–95%	77–80%	• Deeper breathing than at Zone 2 • Slightly higher sense of leg or arm fatigue than Zone 2 • Comfortably solid • Conversation is start-stop in nature • Close to marathon pace (flat/road) • Half Ironman pace is normally in this zone • 3-8 hour effort
4	Sub-threshold	16–18 Hard	96–99% (LTHR)	81–83%	• This hurts • Lactate threshold training • Conversation difficult to hold (almost impossible due to depth and frequency of breathing) • Continuous sense of leg or arm fatigue and concentration required to maintain effort • The top marker of this zone is your threshold heart rate (your average heart rate for a 1-hour all-out effort, i.e. a 1-hour bike or run time trial) • As fitness increases this intensity can be more easily maintained • Approx. half marathon to 10km pace (flat/road) depending on runner's pace • Olympic-distance triathlon effort • 1-3 hour effort

Zone	Effort	RPE (rate of perceived exertion)	% of LTHR (lactate threshold heart rate)	% of maximum heart rate	Zone information and descriptors
5a	Above threshold (super threshold)	18 Very hard	100–102%	84–85%	• This really hurts. The effort starts hard and progresses to uncomfortable very quickly. • Conversation not possible • VO2 Max training • 3km–5km pace (flat/road) depending on runner's pace. Elite 10km runner race pace (sub 1 hour) • Sprint-distance triathlon pace (under 1 hour) • 20 minutes – 1 hour effort
5b	Aerobic capacity	19	103–106%	86–89%	• Conversation not possible • VO2 Max training • 2-20 minute time trial pace
5c	An-aerobic capacity	20	107–110+%	90–95%	• Very short, high intensity effort • Sprints • Less than 2-minute efforts

Both % of threshold heart rate and maximum heart rate have been provided, as some people have a preference for one over the other. It is my belief that threshold heart rate is a superior form of measurement, as understanding your intensity level in relation to this key marker is more beneficial to the athlete than understanding intensity relative to maximum heart rate. The reason for this is because it is your output at threshold that is a key determining factor of your success compared to what your maximum heart rate is.

*LTHR, Maximum HR Zones courtesy of Joe Friel, creator of Training Peaks

https://www.trainingpeaks.com/blog/joe-friel-s-quick-guide-to-setting-zones/

Time-based guidelines adapted from *Total Heart Rate Training – Customize and maximize your workout using a heart rate monitor* by Joe Friel, Ulysses Press, 2006

YOUR ZONES

When you look at the table, you'll see that the zones are listed down the left-hand side, and the different ways of identifying them are listed across the top. The table is about keeping things simple, so we use the terms Zone 1, Zone 2, Zone 3, and so on, to represent a particular effort level. This is easier than saying tempo, sub-threshold, etc. Sometimes you may see this simplified to Z2, Z4 or Z1/2.

At this point you have an understanding of RPE, heart rate and power, and can start to correlate this with the different zones. There are also markers that you may not be able to use because you haven't yet done the required testing. The final column in the table also has a set of descriptors, and if you're not sure where or how to start assigning your zones, this is the column you should look at. As we go on and continue your Ironman education, you'll be able to identify the zone you're in according to all the different measurements. In other words, you'll be fluent in the language.

There are two big markers to understand in the table. The first is your lactate threshold heart rate. This is the maximum heart rate you could maintain if you were to sustain an all-out effort for exactly one hour – an excruciating experience. If your heart rate is below this marker you are said to be 'below threshold', and above this point you are said to be 'above threshold'. (You probably don't know your lactate threshold at the moment, but don't worry, we'll look at how to identify that in the next chapter.) You will notice that this threshold is the transition from Zone 4 to Zone 5. This is an important marker, and for ease of understanding, zones above this point are referred to as 5a, 5b and 5c. You are well and truly able to work in these zones, but only for periods of less than an hour. For instance in many a 3km, 5km and even a 10km running event, you will operate above your threshold level because you will be running for periods much shorter than one hour. Likewise, in any swimming event or cycling event that lasts less than one hour, you will be working at heart rates, speeds/paces in excess of your lactate threshold.

The second critical marker in the table is your aerobic threshold. This point falls at the top end of Zone 2. For the Ironman athlete this is even more important than the lactate threshold, because it is possible to operate in Zone 2 for hours and hours. However, as you dip into Zone 3 the fatigue on your body is drastically increased. While Zone 3 feels easy at first, performing in this zone will catch up with you towards the end of an Ironman. An athlete that is left spinning into T2 or walking from the 30km mark has not understood their paces and will often have started out at a Zone 3 effort that felt 'easy' rather than starting where they should have at a Zone 2 effort. This will all be discussed in more detail in Chapter 8.

Now it's time for a little exercise to start figuring out your zones. For the following set, you can identify your zones based on the descriptors in the final column of the table. It's a start, and as you continue on your journey you'll continue to refine your understanding of your zones.

YOUR JOURNEY

Let's hit the road so we can better understand how all this works in practice. The following set can be completed on either the bike or run. It provides a great way to help understand your heart rate, RPE and, if using it, power, in each zone.

WARM-UP

10 minutes Zone 1

10 minutes Zone 2

MAIN SET

12 minutes Zone 2

8 minutes Zone 3

6 minutes Zone 4

3 minutes Zone 5b

Complete the above set once for a shorter set and two or three times for a longer set (two or three repetitions). If completing two or three sets, look to include a one-minute walk or spin in between them.

COOL DOWN

10 minutes Zone 1

After completing this set looking at your heart rate or power, try completing it at a later stage *not* looking at your metrics and going completely on RPE or feel. Then, at the conclusion of the second set, review your data to see how you went, both the first time you completed the set and the second or third. In subsequent sets you can even get tricky and check your heart rate monitor during the first set, then not look at it during the second or third repetition – or vice versa. Make sure to review how you went.

A WORD OF CAUTION

It is common for triathletes to start to over-think things. Understand that you are emotionally attached to your training and your event and to how they both go. It's natural that you want to do well; this is completely normal and absolutely fantastic. However, that desire to do well means that triathletes are susceptible to 'pushing things'. If aiming for Zone 2, you might find it becomes Zone 3, or that Zone 4 tips over into Zone 5. You need to be aware, from the outset, that this is not necessarily beneficial. You are an Ironman triathlete, so you need to be spending time swimming, biking and running in Zone 2 to improve your aerobic threshold, and in Zone 4 and up to improve your anaerobic threshold. This means that easy needs to be easy and hard needs to be hard, but you don't have to overdo things. Trust that undertaking the right training, in the right zones, will deliver the results you desire. There are no shortcuts to success.

•◦ •❯ •◦ •❯

At this point your Ironman education is coming together incredibly well. You understand the key terms of aerobic threshold and anaerobic threshold, and why these are vital to the Ironman triathlete and must not be confused with VO2 Max. You have started to develop your own personal intensity chart. You have a guide to your intensity and can start to develop your understanding about RPE at each level. You understand that RPE is the gold standard that the Ironman triathlete must learn to use, but you can use heart rate and power as a guide. In the next chapter, when we start implementing fitness tests, you're going to take this further. We'll do a test to determine your lactate threshold, and you will be able to determine your appropriate heart rate zones from your threshold heart rate.

CHAPTER 4

FITNESS TESTING

In the previous chapter we learnt all about how to measure and assess the intensity of your training by using zones, and these lessons will be revisited when we talk later about pacing. Now I want to move on to another topic – fitness testing. Fitness testing is all about a line in the sand. It is saying that at this point in time, this is what you are capable of doing. It also provides a means of measuring your lactate threshold, which will allow you to use the concept of training zones more accurately and with greater sophistication.

Undertaking a fitness test provides a range of benefits. The first is that it allows you to set important training parameters by establishing your threshold heart rate and threshold power. This can then be used to determine your power and heart rate zones. This is the beauty of the power meter over pace or speed; it takes all factors into consideration and allows you to accurately know your output. The power of the power meter starts to become apparent.

The other reason that a fitness test is beneficial is that you can use the information to determine whether your training is delivering the desired improvements. If your training is not working, then you can look to modify your approach before continuing. Coupled with this, a fitness test creates a reference point for your training year on year. For instance, you are able to compare your fitness between Ironman events. In other words, it gives you a standard measure.

It can be a good idea to undertake a fitness test a few weeks prior to your Ironman race. A danger here is that you might have a poor fitness test, which might crush your confidence. But if you have completed the required training a poor fitness test is highly unlikely, and the benefits that it provides far outweigh the drawbacks. For example, if you have a disaster of a race! What? Surely not! But yes, you could. Despite having all the knowledge and skill, and undertaking all the preparation necessary for a great race, there is still the possibility that you will have a fizzle. Even pros have fizzles! Nutrition, blisters, bike crashes, bike mechanicals, faulty gear, food poisoning – the list of potential disasters that can bring you down is long (and yes, I have heard of each of these occurring to different people in different races). But by collecting data from a fitness test prior to the event, you are in a position to know how you were tracking and the fitness you had.

Another reason to have a fitness test prior to a race is that the nature of Ironman races makes them very difficult to compare. While the distance 3.8/180/42.2km is a standard measure, just as a marathon is a standard measure, an Ironman has much greater variability in terms of the swim conditions, cycling course, running course and temperature when compared to marathons. Some Ironmans are flat, others hilly and some technical, some occur at altitude, some in relentless wind and humidity and others in oppressive heat. This makes it nearly impossible to compare different events, which is why you need the standard nature of a fitness test to properly assess how your fitness compares from one year to another.

TAKING A FITNESS TEST

You can go to a lab to undertake a fitness test and if you're prepared to part with the dough for this, by all means go for it. But experience suggests that the cost and inconvenience of lab testing means that it cannot be performed as regularly as field testing. It can be great once or twice a year to hit the lab and get a formal assessment, but outside the lab the following tests will prove much more useful. They are also completely free, which means you can repeat them as often as you like without cost becoming an issue.

There are a number of ways to undertake a DIY fitness test, but I'm going to suggest one for the swim, one for the bike and one for the run. I'll also discuss two other commonly used options which may be of interest and can be a great way to keep yourself motivated when training. It is beneficial to test in a number of different ways, as this helps provide motivation for your training and also creates a clearer picture of your fitness over time and across each discipline.

The swim test is one that was brought to our attention by the open water swim guru Paul Newsome from Swim Smooth. It involves a 400m and 200m swim test (yes, in that order). The key bike and run test use a method popularised by legendary endurance coach Joe Friel. Of the final two tests discussed, the first looks to determine your aerobic output in each discipline, while the second fitness test provides a lot of fun.

Before you start testing yourself, a word of warning. Don't worry if you don't feel you 'nailed' your fitness test the first time. Understanding how to undertake a fitness test is a learning process in itself. So don't worry; that's part of the journey!

FITNESS TEST 1:
THE SWIMMING FITNESS TEST

The first fitness test that I recommend involves a 400m time trial followed by a 200m time trial. This test is used to determine your critical swim speed and your threshold swim speed. I prefer this test to other swim fitness tests because I find that it provides the most accurate results.

You complete the test by swimming a 400m time trial as fast as you can, having a break and then swimming a 200m time trial. You then put your numbers into a magical CSS calculator, which can be found in the App Store by looking up CSS calculator. Our preference is the 'CSS Calculator Pro'.[8] So download the app, punch in your times, and wham bam you get your critical swim speed.

The test is conducted as follows:

WARM-UP

- 400m as 75m freestyle, 25m backstroke (Zone 1)
- 400m freestyle as 25m hard (Zone 4) 25m easy (Zone 2)
- 200m freestyle as 50m moderate (Zone 3) 50m easy (Zone 2)

MAIN SET

- 400m freestyle time trial

If completing the test on your own, remember to hit the lap key on your watch or alternatively have a friend time your fitness test. If a

---

8   The name of the app may change in the future, so if you can't find it in the App Store search CSS Calculator and find the relevant app.

friend times your test, ask them to take your splits every 100m – this can be very insightful!

Complete the 400m time trial first, going as hard as you can for the 400m.

After finishing this test, complete an easy 300m freestyle. Make sure to keep the blood flowing to the arms and shoulders to clear the lactic acid. Complete the first 100m at a very easy pace, the second 100m at a warm-up pace and the final 100m at a steady pace.

Now complete the 200m freestyle time trial going as hard as you can for the 200m.

COOL DOWN

- 300m easy freestyle (Zone 2)
- 300m as 50m freestyle (Zone 1)/ 50m backstroke (Zone 1)

Once out of the water put your times into the u-beaut calculator and find out your threshold swim pace and your critical swim speed – CSS pace.

FITNESS TEST 2:
THE 30-MINUTE LACTATE THRESHOLD TEST

The aim of this test is to complete an all-out 30-minute time trial; you are cycling or running as hard as you can for the entire 30 minutes of the main set. The test should be conducted on a velodrome, running track, suitable road or venue that is free of obstructions, interruptions and elevation changes. When you're about to commence the test, start a new file on your watch. When you start biking or running, make sure to hit the start button!

The test is conducted as follows and can be completed on the bike or running:

WARM-UP

- 10 minutes easy Zone 1
- 10 minutes steady Zone 2
- 6 x 30-second efforts (Zone 4) on a 30-second (Zone 2) recovery jog or spin[9]
- Finish with 4 minutes Zone 2 cycling or running

Take a couple of minutes to compose yourself before starting your 30-minute fitness test.

MAIN SET

- Start your fitness test; take the first few minutes to build into your fitness test.

- Hit the lap key after 10 minutes or program your watch to trigger an automatic lap at this time interval.

- Continue cycling or running hard for another 20 minutes. At the end of this time (making a total of 30 minutes running) stop the workout.

---

9   This means that you run for 30 seconds at what feels like a Zone 4 pace, followed by 30 seconds at what feels like a Zone 2 pace. Repeat this six times, for a total of six minutes running. Note that heart rate will not fully respond during this time so you will just have to go on RPE.

COOL DOWN

- Complete a cool down of 10–15 minutes easy Zone 1 spinning or running.

ADDITIONAL SET NOTES

- This set should be conducted on flat, un-interrupted terrain.
- Make sure you wear your heart rate monitor for the set.
- Ideally use a circular running or cycling loop, as this helps negate the effect that a windy day would have on the test.
- Note in your training diary any adverse weather conditions, in particular, a hot day.

This fitness test allows you to determine your lactate threshold, and improving the distance travelled in the 30 minutes becomes the ultimate goal of the test. Assuming you have given it your all, your average heart rate for the final 20-minute period of the test is your lactate threshold.[10] Knowing this will help you use the intensity zones table in a more sophisticated way. Grab your calculator, turn to the page with the intensity zones table, and work out what your heart rate and power should be at each zone by calculating the relevant percentage of your lactate threshold heart rate or power.

10   http://www.trainingbible.com/joesblog/2009/11/quick-guide-to-setting-zones.html

FITNESS TEST 3:
THE 60-MINUTE AEROBIC THRESHOLD TEST

Like the 30-minute test, this is best conducted on flat terrain free of obstacles. The aim of this test is to maintain your heart rate or power in Zone 3 for a full hour and travel as far as possible. This is not about cycling or running harder, but being as efficient as possible in this zone.

Similar to the 30-minute fitness test, the goal of this test is to increase the distance that you travel in this 60-minute period; however, in this case you need to aim to do so without increasing your average heart rate. It needs to stay within Zone 3.

The set is conducted as follows:

WARM-UP

- 10 minutes Zone 1
- 5 minutes Zone 2

Take a couple of minutes to compose yourself and grab a drink if needed.

MAIN SET

- 5 minutes to establish a steady Zone 3 heart rate. At the end of 5 minutes hit your lap button, and without stopping continue into:
- 60 minutes Zone 3 cycling or running (while this may sound easy, it will take focus to achieve).
- At the end of the 60 minutes, hit your lap key. Your fitness test is complete.

COOL DOWN

- 10 minutes easy Zone 1 run or spin

ADDITIONAL SET NOTES

- In your diary include both the distance covered during your 60-minute test and also your average heart rate for this time.

- This set should be conducted on flat un-interrupted terrain.

- Make sure you wear your heart rate monitor for the set.

- Ideally use a circular cycling or running loop for the test as this helps negate the effect that a windy day would have on the results.

- Also note into your training diary if there are any adverse weather conditions, in particular, a hot day.

- It helps to mentally break the test up into three 20-minute blocks.

  - Block 1: This is easy.

  - Block 2: This is starting to hurt.

  - Block 3: I'm done now, just make this stop – typically you're mentally exhausted by now.

Now review your file: record your average heart rate, pace, power and total distance. It is also interesting to look at your maximum heart rate and see how close this was to your average heart rate. Ideally, for the 60-minute portion of the main set of your fitness test, your average heart rate and maximum heart rate will be very close if not exactly the same. The closer together these two numbers are, the more consistent you were during your test.

FITNESS TEST 4: THE UPHILL TIME TRIAL

This test is different from the above tests in that it is distance based and your aim is to improve your time. You are aiming to complete your chosen hill or designated portion of the hill as fast as possible. As above, this test can be completed on the bike or running on a hill that suits the chosen discipline.

WARM-UP

- 10 minutes Zone 1 building to Zone 2
- 2 x 3 minutes building over the 3 minutes to Zone 4
- 4 minutes Zone 2 cycling or running

Take a few minutes to compose yourself then start your test.

MAIN SET – THE FITNESS TEST

- Hit your lap key and cycle or run as fast as possible from your start point to your designated end point.

- Keep in mind that your first attempt should take approximately 35–40 minutes, so that it still takes more than 30 minutes once you have improved.

- Remember to keep things in check for the first 3 minutes of the test and build into it from there.

- Upon reaching the top of your chosen hill or your designated end point, hit your lap key.

After completing the test, take a few minutes to compose yourself before undertaking your cool down.

COOL DOWN

Turn and head back down the hill at an easy Zone 1 pace.

ADDITIONAL SET NOTES

- Aim to find a hill that is free of any significant downhill sections.

- Make sure you wear your heart rate monitor for the set.

- Note in your training diary any adverse weather conditions, in particular, a hot day.

For the bike and run, fitness test 1 is essential and the other two are optional. However, the optional two provide a useful way to track training and also provide a lot of fun.

REPEATING FITNESS TESTS

Down the track, when you repeat the fitness tests as outlined above, you need to follow the same parameters. A common mistake among triathletes is to aim to increase their maximum heart rate for subsequent fitness tests, and then use this as a guide for their improvement. But this is *not* what your aim is. After establishing your maximum heart rate and anaerobic threshold heart rate, these points will stay relatively consistent. It is the *pace or power output* that you are able to maintain at these points that you are looking to improve.

☙ ☙ ☙ ☙

Whoosh! You now understand how to undertake an appropriate fitness test for the Ironman triathlete – four in fact – and can determine your anaerobic threshold using the 30-minute fitness test. Along with your understanding of intensity zones, you now have all the knowledge in place to create a pacing plan, which we will discuss in Part 2. Now we're going to move on to another fun fundamental – nutrition and hydration.

CHAPTER 5

FEEDING YOUR FITNESS

Nutrition is often referred to as the hidden discipline; this is because it's often neglected. You can tick every box on your preparation and be exceptionally fit, but if you come unstuck on this one, you will be left walking at the end of your race. This is because you cannot store enough fuel, energy or water on board (within your body) to power you through to the end of your Ironman event. You need to consume these while cycling and running.

If you don't manage to re-fuel and re-hydrate while on the bike and run, you risk hitting the wall! Hitting the wall is when you don't have enough fuel – carbohydrate – on board to meet the energy demands of what you are undertaking. This can cause your pace to plummet on the bike, and bring you to a walk on the run with the feeling that 'I'm simply not fit enough'.

On the other hand, however, you don't want to be eating excessively or eating the incorrect types of foods during your bike or run, as this can lead to gut upset and prevent you from finishing your race. Given that we can't eat too little, we can't eat too much and we have to eat the right types of food, we first need to equip ourselves with some knowledge about what you require.

To understand our nutrition and hydration needs, we first need to understand the following topics: carbohydrate (CHO) and fat as a fuel source, how to read nutrition labels, suitable foods for triathlon, how to plan your nutrition for training, and your hydration needs.

Yes, this topic is involved. However, working through the elements systematically enables your knowledge to grow and build as the concepts begin to relate to each other. By the end of this chapter, you will have a sound understanding around your required nutrition and hydration demands as an Ironman athlete, and how you will go about meeting these needs.

To start, we need to understand the difference between carbohydrate and fat as a fuel source.

CARBOHYDRATE VS. FAT

There is a lot of debate around about carbohydrate compared to fat as a fuel source. To understand what our body requires, we must first understand how it uses each of these substances and its preference for different fuel sources to meet its energy needs in changing conditions.

To the Ironman athlete, both carbohydrate and fat metabolism (the body's way of creating energy) are important pathways that deliver the energy needed to swim, bike and run. You need to supply both pathways with their required fuel so that your body can continue to operate and deliver energy to the working muscles.

The next concept that we need to understand is that our bodies prefer one pathway over the other, depending on the circumstances. The key factor here is that as intensity (how hard you're working) increases, your body prefers to utilise CHO as its primary fuel source.

Your body is still using fat to create energy, but the energy demands you require are above what can be supplied solely from fat metabolism, and as a result your body must find a faster way to create energy. This is why it looks to CHO. At the extreme end of the spectrum, when you're working at intensities in the Zone 5 range, your body is deriving nearly 100% of the required energy from CHO.

We also need to understand that at standard-distance triathlon (1,500m/40km/10km) pace, Half Ironman pace and, for some people, even Ironman pace, you only have enough CHO on board to last about 90–120 minutes.[11] Given we can ballpark your Ironman time at 8–17 hours, you don't have to be a genius to figure out you need to take CHO on board as you compete. I will say it again: during your Ironman you will need to take on board CHO as you compete.[12]

A final concept that we need to understand is that both energy pathways can be trained to improve their efficiency. Just as you can train your muscles to improve your swimming, biking and running, you can also train your body to be better at metabolising food to create energy. It must be stressed here, however, that you cannot train your body to the extreme where it can rely only on fat to deliver your energy needs. As intensity increases your body will have a preference for CHO, whether you like it or not. If you run out of CHO your pace will plummet, and you will be forced to spin or walk because your body cannot deliver the energy requirements from fat fast enough to allow you to sustain a reasonable speed/pace. You have hit the wall!

11   www.sportsdietitians.com.au

12   Apologies – I may get a bit passionate about this topic with all the misinformation flying around!

I also want to emphasise here that a lack of adequate nutrition may affect the quality of your training – not just your racing. If you're left dawdling on your long swim, cycle or run due to hitting the wall, the session won't have the desired training effect. The message here is to practise, refine and improve your understanding of nutrition.

A common question asked at this point is, 'Don't I need to consume fat as well?' This is a great question; however, the body has abundant fat stores that it can access, so there's no need to consume fat during your race. It is just that fat, which contains a huge amount of energy, is difficult for the body to metabolise quickly, so CHO should be the focus of your nutrition.

The classic example of not fuelling properly comes from Julie Moss and her infamous crawl to the finish line of the 1982 Hawaii Ironman. After leading the race she collapsed only metres from the finish line, unable to run any more. While there were a few factors at play here, a large part of this was as a result of inadequate fuelling and inadequate hydration.[13]

UNDERSTANDING CHO OPTIONS

Now that we understand why CHO is so important, we need to understand how to implement this knowledge in your triathlon. The starting point for this understanding is to be able to read food nutrition labels. From there we need to understand appropriate training and racing fuel sources.

13   http://www.Ironman.com/triathlon-news/articles/2003/02/the-most-famous-finish-in-Ironman-history-julie-moss-takes-you-through-her-race.aspx#axzz4nKqPhAnT

To understand the CHO content of foods, you need to look at the label on the back of the packet. We are after high CHO values with low fat and protein values; in other words – we want foods that are high in sugar. Along with this we need to be careful to look at the 'per serving' values and determine how many servings are in the packet or how many servings we are consuming.

A nutrition label may look like this:

NUTRITION LABEL 1

Nutrition information

Servings per package: 1 Serving size 68.37g

	Avg. quantity per serving	Avg. quantity per 100g
Energy	1090kj	1590kj
Protein	0.0g	0.0g
Fat – total	**0.0g**	**0.0g**
-saturated	0.0g	0.0g
Carbohydrate – total (CHO)	**65g**	**94.9g**
-sugars	10g	14.6g
Dietary fibre	0.0g	0.0g
Sodium	500mg	0.73g

NUTRITION LABEL 2

Nutrition information

Servings per package:1   Serving size 55g

	Avg. quantity per serving	Avg. quantity per 100g
Energy	1170kj	2150kj
Protein	3.6g	6.5g
Fat – total	**14.7g**	**27.2g**
-saturated	9.3g	17.1g
Carbohydrate – total (CHO)	**32.4g**	**59.9g**
-sugars	28.5g	52.8g
Dietary fibre	0.0g	0.0g
Sodium	51mg	92mg

In the first packet we see that the food has a high CHO content, while in the second example we see that there is a high fat content relative to the CHO content. Despite both delivering a significant amount of CHO, in this case the first example would be a better food or fuel choice when training or racing. As a general rule you should aim for the fat content to be less than 10%. In the second packet we can clearly see that it's just over 27g per 100g, meaning it's almost 27% and a less suitable food.

Keep in mind that these are the types of food that we recommend you consume while training and racing, and do not form a part of your everyday balanced diet. Outside of training and racing you should be including quality protein, fats, carbohydrate and fibre in your diet, and eating an abundance of fresh fruit and vegetables.

Your daily diet is a whole topic of its own, and well beyond the scope of what we can cover here.[14]

Some of the foods that are best suited to Ironman triathlon include:

- White bread sandwiches with honey, jam or, for the Aussies, Vegemite
- Wraps with spreads similar to the above
- Coke and soft drink (diluted with water)
- Sports drinks that contain a CHO component, but be careful, as some are purely electrolyte and don't contain any CHO. Likewise, diet drinks won't contain any CHO.
- Sports bars
- Gels
- Bananas or any fruit
- Rice crisps
- Sesame snaps
- Lollies or candy
- Muesli bars – low-fat versions
- Fruit bread, fruit buns and, around Easter, hot cross buns!

---

14 If nutrition is a deep concern for you, consider contacting an Accredited Practicing Dietitian (APD) with expertise in nutrition for endurance events. The national sports dietitians association in your country should be able to find suitable APDs with a special interest in endurance events. USA: www.scandpg.org Europe: www.essna.com UK: www.senr.org.uk Canada: www.dietitians.ca Australia: www.sportsdietitians.com.au

TRAINING FOODS VS. RACING FOODS

Many triathletes like variety in what they're eating. The above list helps with this; however, what we can tolerate in training and racing may be different. When training, due to the shorter duration and lower overall stress placed on your body, you can tolerate foods that may not be as well suited to race day. In training you can eat foods that are higher in fibre and may be more difficult to consume. When it comes to race day, however, we want foods that are easy to carry, easy to consume and low in fibre. We want the foods to be low in fibre as this makes them easier for the body to digest, meaning they're less likely to cause gut upset.

Naturally, we do need to train on our 'race foods' to check that we can tolerate them and they work for us. After your preferred race foods have been identified, you can leave your racing foods till the final six to eight weeks of your training plan and stick with 'training foods' prior to this time. This helps prevent you from getting bored of the foods you will use on race day. The other benefit is that often these 'training' foods are more economical than a continuous flow of expensive gels, sports bars and sports drinks.

I'm not a fan of gels, to say the least, but love fruit bread, the convenience of muesli bars and the economical choice of lollies. I am fortunate that I have trained and raced on gels and sports drinks, and know what agrees with me and what I can tolerate. As such, I will save these foods for the training period just before race day (six to eight weeks) and race day itself. Conversely, on race day I'm reluctant to use lollies, muesli bars or fruit bread, as they can be challenging to consume and I find them harsh on my stomach under race conditions.

TROUBLESHOOTING

Now that we have some understanding of CHO and food choices, we need to pull all this information together. It's important to practise nutrition in training so that you have the knowledge you need to be flexible with your food choices when racing. In a race you will push yourself harder than in training because the distance or time collectively spent competing is longer. This increase in the stress placed on the body can lead to gut upset, even if you haven't experienced this in training. This gut upset can present itself in a number of ways, the most common being:

- A stitch
- Sloshing
- Bloating
- Inability to eat
- Diarrhoea

We need to plan and aim to prevent the worst of this. Some gastro intestinal (GI) upset is normal, even among those who have exceptional races – come race day everybody is pushing their body beyond what they normally do. Experienced racers understand how to deal with these types of challenges and prevent the worst of them happening so that it doesn't affect their swimming, cycling or running. Soon you will have this understanding too.

First you need to understand the two common reasons why GI upset occurs in races more than in training. As mentioned, you will push yourself further and possibly harder in a race than you would in training. When swimming, cycling or running hard your body shunts blood to the working muscles in your legs and to your heart. To aid this it decreases blood supply to the non-vital organs of your stomach and digestive system. The reduced blood flow makes it harder for your body to absorb the digested food. A potential result of this is GI upset, presenting in the various ways outlined above. One way to help relieve this is to slow your pace temporarily to allow your body to 'process' the fuel or food before returning to your previous cycling or running pace.

The second common cause of gut upset in a race is consuming CHO at too high a concentration for your stomach. This means your body cannot absorb what you have consumed. The maximum level of CHO concentration that sports drinks should contain is 8%, but ideally they should have a concentration less than this – generally around 6%.[15] Gels have a concentration much higher than this, which is why you always need to drink water when you consume a gel.

If you experience sloshing while running or indeed cycling, this is often (though not always) a result of having a CHO concentration above 6–8% in your stomach. The solution to this is to have water, slow your pace and allow the feeling to subside and gastric emptying to occur. Then you need to return to consuming your planned nutrition or you will risk hitting the wall later! A common error among new and less experienced triathletes is not realising that Coke has a CHO concentration of 10% – well above the 6% your gut can tolerate. When having Coke you need to treat it like a gel and have water with it to help dilute the concentration.

15   https://www.sportsdietitians.com.au/wp-content/uploads/2015/04/Sports-Drinks.
      pdf Accessed 24 March 2017

HOW MUCH?

Now that you understand the CHO content of foods, the next question to ask is how much CHO should you consume? Again, this is a question that is different for every individual and will require you to practise in your long training sets. There are, however, some guidelines that will help determine what your CHO requirements should be. As a guide, in competition you should aim for 50–90g CHO per hour, while in training you can aim for slightly less than this – 40–75g per hour is recommended.[16]

The next step is to formulate a nutrition plan. This should happen in a basic format for each long training set (greater than two hours) you undertake, as this is when you equip yourself with the nutrition knowledge you need to have on race day. This knowledge, along with your plan, allows you to be flexible if needed. When it comes to nutrition, failing to plan is planning to fail.

This is how you do it:

1. Work out the number of hours that you anticipate you will cycle or run for.

2. Work out the amount of CHO you would like to consume per hour (50–90g for racing and around 40–75g in 'normal' training, i.e. not when you are practising your race nutrition).

3. Lay out your nutrition for each hour in a separate pile.

---

16   Suzanne Girard Eberle, MS, RDN, CSSD, *Endurance Sports Nutrition – Fuel your body for optimal performance*, 3rd edn, Human Kinetics, 2014

4. Over time you will develop an understanding of how much food you need to consume per hour and what the different CHO values of foods are.

With the above procedure in place, along with practise, refinement and improvement through training, you will hit the start line of your race confident that you will be able to work your way through any nutrition challenges you encounter.

NUTRITION ON THE BIKE VS. ON THE RUN

At this time it is also important that we look at nutrition on the bike compared to on the run. Being on the bike allows greater freedom with your nutrition and thus we want to make sure we utilise this opportunity. There are two main points to consider. Firstly, it is easier to carry particular types of nutrition with you on the bike compared to the run and, secondly, it is easier to consume that nutrition on the bike.

Let's start with the carrying differences. With the ability to use on-bike storage, bulky items are much easier to carry. As a result you may opt to use sports bars or other larger nutrition items as part of your overall nutrition strategy. Such an approach is beneficial for many triathletes, as it allows a greater range in what they consume; in particular, allowing them to consume solid foods early and save the use of gels for later in their race.

The second carrying benefit is the use of your bike bottles or bidons. As these are easy to carry on the bike compared to on the run, you are able to carry a personalised sports drink mix instead of having to rely on on-course nutrition. This approach allows you to consume a concentrated but pre-determined mix – one that you know agrees with you and one that you have complete confidence in. Generally the best option for triathletes is to use a combination of the above strategies. Rely on some solid foods and some concentrated sports drink mix.

The second advantage of the bike is the ability to consume a higher concentration of CHO. The reasons for this are because there is a lower jostling effect on the bike and a lower sustained heart rate. These two factors, along with the fact that the accumulated fatigue of the race is lower on the bike leg, mean you are less likely to experience gut upset or GI issues while riding.

With this in mind we are able to consume CHO at concentrations of 10-20g more than you would later in the race when running. Such an approach works beautifully because it ensures that you hit the start of the run with a full fuel tank, rather than one which is running on empty or only half full. You have done the hard work of consuming nutrition early rather than waiting for problems to develop that you have to try to solve. This also allows you to negate some of the deficit that was created through not being able to consume nutrition during the swim.

As with everything, we need to practise our nutrition in training to ensure its success come race day. Let's look at how we go about it.

NUTRITION IN TRAINING

When training, you will need to consume some carbohydrate on training sessions of two hours or longer; under this duration most people can happily finish their set. That said, however, some people might choose to take something light to eat. Beyond two hours, nutrition becomes a necessity. As you have learnt, the intensity at which you are training is going to influence your nutritional needs. Given that training sets are often completed at a lower intensity and for shorter durations than your Ironman event, this means that your nutrition requirements are not as pronounced. With this in mind, in training you're going to shoot for 40–75g of CHO per hour.

This leaves us in a predicament, however, because you still need to practise your race day nutrition *in training*. Our recommendation is that over the final six to eight weeks of training, when your long bike sessions and runs are significant, you undertake your planned race nutrition for a portion or portions of your set. For instance, if aiming for 50g per hour in training and 75g per hour when racing, your nutrition plan for a morning run lasting 3 hours might look something like this:

0–1.5 HOURS: no need to consume CHO as you have just had breakfast.

1.5–2.5 HOURS: consume CHO at race quantity on planned race foods – approximately 75g per hour.

2.5–3 HOURS: no requirement for nutrition.

Note that you don't need any nutrition in the last segment. This is because the time taken for digestion and transport from the stomach to muscles is about 30 minutes. This means that CHO consumed within the last half hour will not make it to the working muscles in time to be utilised. This is the reason that, if you do ever hit the wall, you'll have to wait about 30 minutes after consuming food for the effects of feeling sluggish to wear off. Keep in mind, however, that if you have a brick set (bike and run set – discussed in Chapter 7) you will still need to consume CHO over the last 30 minutes of your cycle – after all, your training set will not be finishing till your run is over.

Now let's look at a nutrition plan for a training set lasting five hours:

0-1 HOUR: no need to consume CHO as you have just had breakfast.

1-2 HOURS: consume foods totalling 40g of CHO.

2-5 HOURS: consume CHO at race quantity on planned race foods – approximately 75g per hour. In this case, being a longer set, the athlete is choosing to consume their race CHO content through to the conclusion of the cycle.

A WORD OF CAUTION

When consuming CHO at rates above 60g per hour, you need to include CHO from different sources, with the additional source generally being fructose. The reason different CHO sources are needed is because of the way in which CHO is transported across the gut – the two different types of sugars need different types of transport mechanisms to make the trip. Your body only has enough transport mechanisms to transport CHO in the form of glucose or maltodextrin (two common CHO sources) across the gut wall at a rate of 60g of CHO per hour. However, the mechanisms responsible for transporting fructose are sitting around twiddling their thumbs, waiting for something do. So, it makes sense to include fructose as well. It's like travelling between two cities. If the train is full, but the bus is already there and is going to be running whether you jump on it or not, you might as well use it. The transporters in the body for fructose are like the bus; they're already present and ready to take more CHO across your gut wall.

Given the bus is there, why not use it? This is why you will sometimes hear sports nutrition companies plug a 2:1 ratio; they're referring to the ratio of the glucose/maltodextrin to fructose in the product. But beware of too much of a good thing. The fructose bus has fewer seats than the glucose train. If you try to put too much fructose on the bus it has nowhere to go and is simply left behind. When it comes to your body, fructose being left behind in this manner means just one thing – it has to go out the back. Unfortunately that means diarrhoea! Eek!

HYDRATION – YOUR OIL

Do you remember Julie Moss and her undignified crawl across the finish line of the 1982 Ironman triathlon that I mentioned earlier? Well, while Julie Moss managed to finish her race, others such as Chris Legh did not. At the 1997 Hawaii Ironman World Championships, Chris collapsed 50m from the finish line while in fifth place. While Chris was undoubtedly running on an empty tank, it was severe dehydration that nearly caused his death and meant part of his large intestine had to be removed.[17] I don't want anything like that happening to you.

If food is your fuel, then water is the oil. The amount of sweat that you lose when training is often both misunderstood and underestimated. This is because you don't always *see* your sweat; it evaporates too quickly. Have you ever walked into a cool house or shop on a hot day after you've been cycling or running, only to find yourself dripping wet? This happens because you're still sweating, but the sweat

---

17 http://www.active.com/triathlon/articles/chris-legh-s-tips-on-avoiding-an-Iron-man-bonk, by Ryan Wood. Accessed 26 April 2017

is no longer evaporating. This gives you an indication of just how much sweat you lose that you are blissfully unaware of.

I once worked with an athlete who entered a hot and humid race in Taiwan. Towards the end of the race he was not running well. It was stifling on the course, with no shade and a belting sun. He was clearly dehydrated, and that in turn affected his nutrition. It was like a one, two, knockout punch. It had gone from a case of aiming for a top time to an exercise in survival. At each aid station, he drenched himself in water to try to get rid of the excess heat. But he couldn't move the heat because he was dehydrated. This was an athlete who was light and normally liked to run in the heat, and he was suffering! He finished a respectable fifth in his age group, crossed the line and slumped on the ground in the foetal position. Despite being an experienced racer, this course had eaten him up and spat him out! Upon finally being asked if he needed to go to the medical tent, he readily agreed. The result: two IV drips before colour was restored to his face.

That athlete was me. Even with all the knowledge and experience that I have, and understanding this subject inside and out, I can still get it wrong. I can still make mistakes. There were a range of factors at play that day that contributed to the situation, but those factors were the same for every racer and I accept the decisions and choices I made. The point here is that hydration and nutrition are vital and linked. Despite having a great training plan and being super fit, if you stuff up these important factors you stuff up your race; you won't achieve your personal best and you might not even finish the race.

HOW MUCH HYDRATION?

A drop in hydration of as little as 2% is shown to affect performance, and at 5% dehydration becomes dangerous, so you need to know how to prevent its onset. A good starting point is to know your personal sweat rates. When running, a sweat rate can vary up to 2.3 litres per hour under high intensity exercise in extreme conditions. Luckily, when completing your Ironman you're not going to be running, swimming or cycling at this intensity! But we need to be mindful of the fact that we are still working hard and sweating. Most athletes will need about 590ml of fluid per hour, but this will vary according to a range of factors: wind, temperature, humidity and your personal competing intensity, to name a few.[18]

Conducting a sweat test will give you a guide to your personal sweat rates. This can also be used to determine the amount of salt that you lose through your sweat. We recommend seeing an accredited practising sports dietitian should you wish to have a sweat test conducted.

You can also weigh yourself to get an indication of your sweat rates. To achieve this, weigh yourself before you start to exercise, then complete your cycle or run and weigh yourself again. Make sure you wear the same clothes and be sure to wring them all out, including your socks. You need to do this because this sweat has already left your body, and you need to know how much weight you have lost in terms of sweat. Note if there is any difference between the two weights. You also need to note how much fluid you consumed while you cycled or ran. Add the difference between your starting weight

18 Suzanne Girard Eberle, MS, RDN, CSSD, *Endurance Sports Nutrition – Fuel your body for optimal performance*, 3rd edn, Human Kinetics, 2014

and final weight to the amount of fluid you consumed while training, and you have your sweat rate. This rate is only valid for the temperature, humidity, intensity and discipline that you were training at on that day, but if you do this test several times and under varying conditions, it gives you a good guide to your anticipated high-end and low-end sweat rate, and therefore how much fluid you need to be consuming when you're exercising in that discipline, at that intensity and in those conditions.

This probably leaves you wondering how much you should be drinking. The answer is enough to protect you from dehydration, but not so much that you induce hyponatremia. Say what? Hyponatremia occurs when the sodium levels in the body become unbalanced. Low sodium levels in the blood can be a result of a combination of sweat loss, which decreases the sodium in the body, and over-hydration, which dilutes an already lowered sodium level. People with hyponatremia generally weigh more at the end of a race than at the start because their body is 'holding on' to the water. In triathletes this generally occurs because the athlete is too enthusiastic with their rehydration. They have been told they have to drink water so that they don't become dehydrated, and take things a little too far. This can be exacerbated when the athlete fails to use an electrolyte solution, such as Gatorade, Powerade or similar. The electrolyte component of these drinks means that your body tops up the sodium it has lost through sweat. So when it comes to hydration for an endurance event, you need to ensure that you are replacing the sodium you're losing, and not rehydrating just by drinking water. Absolutely you can drink water, but not *only* water. And if in doubt, drink an electrolyte sports drink.

Phew, this sounds complex doesn't it! Let's now tie it all together. You can't drink too little, and you can't drink too much. So what do you do? Aim to replace only the sweat that you're losing and not more, and ensure that some of the fluid replaced contains an electrolyte. If in doubt, go for the electrolyte.[19]

MANAGING YOUR HYDRATION

Another point that we need to cover relates to nutrition and hydration in hot and cold weather. In order to manage your nutrition and hydration in differing weather conditions, we recommend that you keep your intake of each separate, or at least have a buffer. If you rely on your hydration to get your CHO intake, then you risk hitting the wall down the track. Let me explain...

Let's assume that you enter a race and the weather is forecast to be hot. You know that you need to drink 750ml of fluid an hour, so you tackle this by going with an all-in-one sports drink. The first hour of the cycle rolls by, and despite a warm forecast maximum the temperature remains cool. It turns out you only needed to drink 400ml and your nutrition plan is now out the window!

We need to build in a buffer and take this into consideration. You need to understand that hydration and nutrition, while linked, are separate entities. Any fluid that contains your required CHO needs to be drunk in the period of time allotted for that CHO, or you risk throwing your nutrition out. For example, you might determine that in the first hour you needed to drink 700ml of fluid to obtain your

19 https://www.gssiweb.org/en/sports-science-exchange/article/sse-88-hyponatre-mia-in-athletes

60g of CHO (your hydration and nutrition are completely linked), but you only drink 350ml of fluid because it was cool. You have met your hydration needs, but not your CHO needs – you're now 30g down on your intended intake and you're only an hour into your cycle! This is where it's good to have a buffer to prevent this from occurring. Think: nutrition first (this includes fluid containing nutrition) then water or electrolyte to supplement and top off your hydration.

You will notice that we have discussed everything with time as the reference, not distance. It's much better to use time to guide your nutrition, as this is the critical factor. This way, if you're slower or quicker over a given distance, it won't affect your nutrition plan.

The final concept that you need to be aware of is the 'drip-feed' system. Look to maintain a continuous, steady flow of nutrition and hydration. A small, continuous flow is much easier for your body to deal with and results in you feeling better while you cycle and run. Avoid getting to the end of an hour or into an aid station and having all your nutrition at once. You don't need to be exact to the gram and millilitre – there is some room for give and take – but at the conclusion of a given hour you will want to have consumed approximately 'xyz' CHO and approximately 'xyz' millilitres of fluid.

YOUR JOURNEY

Now that you have solid nutrition and hydration knowledge, you need to experiment with different strategies in your training. Depending on the length of your current sets, look to implement the following:

1. Undertake a sweat test or weigh yourself before and after cycling and running to establish your high-end and low-end sweat rates.

2. Ensure you are consuming sufficient CHO on sets exceeding two hours.

3. Experiment with different food options to determine suitable training and racing foods, and develop your understanding around the CHO content of different foods.

4. Ensure you map out your planned nutrition for your long bike and run sets; it is recommended you plan it in one-hour blocks.

5. On your long sets, implement periods when you incorporate your planned race day nutrition to ensure it works for your needs. Modify this as needed in subsequent sets.

6. If you feel you need additional help with this, book in to see an accredited practising sports dietitian with a special interest in endurance events.

Bam! We have just bombarded your brain with a crash course in sports nutrition and hydration. You now have a firm grasp on the role of CHO and fat in metabolism and the body's preference for CHO as the intensity increases. You understand that there is a limited supply of CHO in the body and know the types of foods best suited to replace this. You know how much CHO you need to consume when cycling and running, and understand the need for mapping out your nutrition, both in training and when racing. You understand hydration requirements and why it's important not to get dehydrated when racing. Implementing these lessons and concepts will ensure that your training improves. You will feel better before, during and after training, and be able to swim, bike and run strongly for your entire race because your body has the necessary fuel and fluid on board to power you through. You are a nutrition and hydration queen ... or king! If you feel a little overwhelmed at this stage, don't worry – that is quite normal. As you implement your newly acquired knowledge in your training, you will increase your confidence in this area. As Benjamin Franklin said, 'Tell me and I forget, teach me and I may remember, involve me and I learn.'

PART 2

TRAINING TECHNIQUES

Okay, I promise you that all the heavy science stuff is now over. But I'm glad you ploughed your way through everything, because now you have a fantastic understanding of the important fundamentals that will underpin not just your training, but racing your best Ironman and qualifying for Kona!

In this second part of the book you're going to hit the ground running – literally; well, cycling and swimming too! You'll learn all about the different training sets that will ultimately form the content of the training plans that are discussed in Part 3. Next we'll move on to the specific techniques that you need to undertake the ultimate challenge

– completing your best Ironman and crossing the finishing line feeling like you're on top of the world. Finally there's a whole chapter devoted to the all-important topic of pacing, and the heavy work we did in Part 1 means you'll be able to understand where this is coming from and how to build it into your training. Right then, let's get to it.

CHAPTER 6

TRAINING SETS

Earlier in the book you developed your understanding around intensity and how to establish your training zones from a fitness test. The next topic that we need to understand is the different training sets that can be used to improve your swim, bike and run fitness. You need to understand what the different sets are, the benefits that they provide and how to 'complete or train' the different sets. Your understanding around intensity zones gains greater relevance here, as it provides a common language that allows us to discuss the effort and intensity required in the training sets.

If you choose not to employ the following training sets and triathlon training methods, you risk not having developed a strong enough aerobic engine to power you through your full Ironman. You also run the risk of not having the leg strength required to finish your Ironman running strong! You want to finish strong, right? For this you are going to need an insane aerobic engine and highly developed body strength, in particular leg strength, to get you 3.8km through the water and over the 222km of bitumen that will line your way!

The training sets that you need to understand are:

- Long swim, bike and run
- Interval session
- Fartlek session
- Tempo session

- Recovery session
- Just-for-fun session

It is essential that you have a well-balanced Ironman training program. This means including the above sessions at strategic times – simply going out for an easy or moderate training session each time you train is not the quickest or most time-effective way to improve your fitness. You also need to understand how to complete a thorough warm-up and an appropriate cool down. At the end of this book you'll find the appendices with all this variety packed into an uber-detailed training program, but for now I want to continue with your education and make sure you know how to nail each of these sets.

THE WARM-UP & COOL DOWN

A warm-up and cool down are an essential part of any training set. A warm-up involves easy swimming, biking or running at the start of a set while gradually building your intensity. Part of the warm-up may include segments of harder training interspersed with segments of easier training.

You need to complete a warm-up because it prepares your body and mind for the session ahead. There are many changes that take place in your body during the warm-up, but the most important ones can be summarised as follows:

- Increased blood temperature, allowing oxygen to more easily bind to the red blood cells.

- Improved blood flow to the working muscles and away from non-essential functions.

- Improved elasticity of the muscles, helping to decrease the risk of injury.

At the end of your warm-up, you should have a light sweat and be mentally and physically ready for the session ahead.

There are a number of ways to complete a succinct and effective warm-up. Having six standard options works well, two for each discipline, as once they're learnt you don't have to think too much about your warm-up. This allows you to relax and enjoy your training. If training in the morning, all you have to do is simply smell the roses or embrace the lovely chlorine cologne of the pool, while training in the afternoon means you can escape the stress of the day.

The main thing with each of the following warm-ups is that you don't want to feel the need to 'push' the pace during this time. Let your swimming, running and riding come to you naturally as you warm up. When it's cold, you will notice that it takes longer for your core temperature to rise and therefore longer for this pace to feel natural. No surprises there, right? ☺

Each of the following warm-ups is paired with a specific training set.

WARM-UP 1 – LONG OR STEADY STATE, SWIM, RIDE AND RUN

BIKE AND RUN

10 minutes easy Zone 1 training.
10 minutes building from Zone 1 to Zone 2, allowing you to naturally build to Zone 2 and into your steady state ride or run.

SWIM

While the above set works well for the bike and run, it needs to be modified for the pool, using the same principle, as follows:

400m easy freestyle and backstroke – 75m freestyle, 25m backstroke

300m easy Zone 1 freestyle

200m freestyle – 75m Zone 2, 25m easy Zone 1

100m steady Zone 2 freestyle

If your swimming experience/pace is slower, this warm-up may be modified by taking 50m off each section so the distances would become: 350m, 250m, 150m and 50m. This gives an approximate time of 15-20 minutes. Again, these distances could be modified further down or up, depending on the experience of the swimmer.

WARM-UP 2 – INTERVAL SET WARM-UP

BIKE AND RUN

10 minutes easy Zone 1 cycling or running, allowing you to naturally build to Zone 2 at the conclusion.

4 x 1-minute efforts:

- These are completed on a 1-minute Zone 2 recovery: i.e. you cycle or run hard for 1 minute, then run at an easy pace or spin for 1 minute, taking 8 minutes in total.

- You will likely find that on the first two you reach a Zone 3 level, and on the final two you approach a Zone 4 level.

2 minutes Zone 2 cycling or running to finish.

SWIM

Again, the above times work well for the bike and run, but need to be modified for the pool using the same principle, as follows:

400m easy freestyle and backstroke – 75m freestyle, 25m backstroke

400m freestyle – 25m hard, 25 easy

200m easy Zone 2 freestyle

Again, these distances can be modified down or up depending on the ability of the swimmer to give approximately 15-20 minutes swimming in total.

WARM-UP 3 – FARTLEK WARM-UP

BIKE AND RUN

10 minutes easy Zone 1 running, allowing yourself to naturally build towards Zone 2 at the conclusion.

2 x 3-minute builds (building your pace over the three minutes from Zone 2 towards a Zone 4 effort).

4 minutes easy Zone 2 running.

SWIM

The above warm-up can be modified for the swim as follows:

400m easy freestyle and backstroke – 75m freestyle, 25m backstroke.

2 x 200m builds, gradually increasing your pace over the 200m to a Zone 4 effort. This can easily be achieved by swimming at Zone 1 for the first 50m, Zone 2 for the next 50m, etc. Complete these on

a 10-second rest interval.

200m steady Zone 2 swimming.

Again, shift distances up or down depending on swimmer ability to give approximately 15-20 minutes total.

COOL DOWN

It's important that you don't overlook the cool down. You complete a cool down to prevent the blood and associated by-products of exercise from pooling in the muscles. Your aim is to gradually return the body to a pre-exercise state. Rather than seeing the cool down as the conclusion of the session, look at it as a means of ensuring you train well in your next session. This little mindset shift makes a big difference to how triathletes view the cool down.

To prevent confusion, the cool down should be kept super-simple and consistent.

At the end of a long endurance set, a cool down is as easy as completing five minutes Zone 1 swimming, cycling or running. If the cool down is at the conclusion of a set that included intensity block(s), ten minutes of easy Zone 1 swimming, cycling or running is recommended.

When swimming, a cool down consists of 400-500m of easy freestyle and backstroke – 50m freestyle and 50m backstroke. If you find backstroke challenging, consider using your pull buoy for the entirety of the cool down.

THE LONG SWIM, RIDE AND RUN

The long endurance session is your most important training session of the week. Not surprisingly, it's generally the favourite training session of the Ironman triathlete, which is fantastic. The long session is the set that most closely relates to the demands of the Ironman triathlete. It is, as it sounds, long and steady. This session will:

- Improve your aerobic energy systems and Ironman body.

- Improve your muscular endurance (swimming, cycling and running strong).

- Allow you to develop long-distance pace awareness.

- Allow you to practise your race nutrition.

- Help to develop your Ironman triathlon mindset, preparing you for the challenge ahead.

- Provide an opportunity to focus and improve in additional areas, such as gear use, basic bike mechanics (puncture repair, fixing a dropped chain – chances are these will happen at some stage in training), uphills, downhills, bike-handling skills and cadence work.

- Get you used to spending long periods of time exercising and long periods of time in the saddle!

The specifics of the long swim, bike and run are determined by how the session is structured and what its objectives are. It is also important, when planning sessions, that we keep our end goal in mind. So we're going to use the maximum cut-off times of the Ironman as our guide – although we are, of course, confident that you won't be at this end of the spectrum! The swim cut-off for Ironman is 2 hours 20 minutes, the bike cut-off is 8 hours 10 minutes and the run cut-off is 6 hours 30 minutes – 17 hours in total. We can easily see that the time spent swimming is much shorter than the time spent running, and both are shorter than the time spent cycling. This ratio should therefore be replicated in the training program, where the long swim is shorter than the long run, and both are shorter than the long bike.

Consequently, at the start of a training program, the long swim may be as little as 60 minutes, and at the upper end the long bike may be 5+ hours. While the long session will often be a steady Zone 1/2 effort, at times efforts at higher zones may be incorporated.

It's recommended that you only increase the distance or duration of any one set by increments of 10%. So a triathlete running 80 minutes can extend this to 88 minutes the following week, and a 180-minute bike ride can be extended by 18 minutes to 198 minutes the following week. While in a strict sense this is okay, you also need to be aware of the training load that has occurred through the week, both in one discipline and across disciplines. How this load progression is implemented will become much clearer when training plans are discussed in Part 3.

INTERVAL SESSION

The interval session is all about hard to very hard training – Zone 4 and above – followed by periods of recovery.

Zone 4 interval training is a staple of the Ironman triathlete, despite Zone 4 being far in excess of the speed maintained on race day. It is at this point that lactate threshold is being taxed, but because the pace maintained is slightly *below* threshold, a larger amount of 'work' can be achieved than when the body is tipped *above* threshold.

Intervals of Zone 5 training are also used, as this type of training creates improvements in the mitochondria make-up of the cells. (The mitochondria are the site of energy production in the body.) In simpler terms, a little bit of high intensity work goes a long way to improving your body's capacity to make energy – that is, it makes you fitter.

It's important to note that high-end Zone 5 training is used sparingly, and it's not the improvement in discipline-specific speed that you're after, but the heart rate response. That means that you shouldn't be 'pushing' – you must always be swimming, biking and running in control and with good form. Heart rate will naturally respond to hard training.

Triathletes should regularly complete these sessions on hills, which provide added strength endurance and reduce the risk of injury. This is discussed in depth in the next chapter. The time period of these intervals is often longer (10 to 30 minutes) than what a pool swimmer, criterium cyclist or road marathoner would be used to, and as such the pace maintained is lower. This allows the cumulative time spent 'working' to be higher, and thus is more closely related to the Ironman triathlete's requirements.

The recovery period of the interval session is essential, as the physical and mental demands of this high intensity training are very challenging, particularly *outside* race conditions. In a traditional interval set the rest period is stationary; however, since training techniques and the understanding of training has improved, it has been found that completing this recovery as an easy spin or a walk into a slow jog is better. This is beneficial because it helps to keep the blood flowing to the legs and the heart rate slightly elevated, which improves the quality of the following interval. Unfortunately this is hard to achieve in the pool in a strict interval session, and so a stationary rest must suffice.

Finally, it's important to note that, no matter your ability, you should build into these sessions. If you have a history of injury or are recovering from an injury, it is recommended that you skip these segments until you can complete them safely.

FARTLEK SESSION

Fartlek means 'speed play' in Swedish, and a fartlek session is when you vary your speed as you train. This could be through a range of speeds or just a few, with segments of hard training followed by segments of easier training.

The key difference between an interval and a fartlek session is the speed at which the 'recovery' portion of the training is completed. In intervals we are moving almost for the sake of moving during the recovery period, because the intense component was, well ... intense. But with a fartlek set, the speed held during the recovery period is much quicker, with an active recovery normally in Zone 2 or higher.

Like an interval session, a fartlek session can be completed in any discipline. However, the higher pace of the recovery portion means that the effort portion of a fartlek session must be completed at either a lower intensity or reduced duration, as compared to an interval session. As a triathlete you achieve a fartlek ride, or something close to it, on almost every hilly long ride you do, as hills naturally cause this effect on your bike.

A key mistake that newer triathletes make is that they focus solely on making the distance, and remove interval and fartlek training from their weekly program. As a result their fitness does not improve as quickly as it would if they retained this type of training.

The fartlek and interval sessions are a fantastic way to train. Due to the increased demands placed on your body for short periods, they are more effective at improving your fitness than just going out for an easy or moderate swim, bike or run set. Therefore, a session that features changes in intensity becomes your second most important training set of the week, with the long session being the most important.

TEMPO SESSION

The tempo session relates to the tempo zone (Zone 3). This is the zone Ironman triathletes love: comfortably solid; controlled, calm efficiency. It's fast so that you feel you're training well, but not so fast that you're uncomfortable, as you might be at a Zone 4 or Zone 5 effort. Due to the lower intensity, large blocks of time can be achieved. This is often the zone you will find yourself in when climbing hills. There are a number of ways in which this session can be structured in your training, allowing the tempo session to occur on the flat or on hills.

Due to the good feeling associated with working in this zone, it's important to make sure the speed of a long ride and run, or even a recovery session, does not creep above Zone 2 (unless specifically stated). Too much time at a Zone 3 pace can lead to over-training. This means you may be too fatigued to hit higher zones during your interval and fartlek sessions as you have wiped yourself out during your long sessions.

RECOVERY & STEADY STATE SETS

The recovery set and steady state set are very similar in nature to the weekly long set; however, the focus of the session and the cumulative time taken are vastly different. This is why they need to be discussed separately. It's also helpful for these sessions to have a different name – this helps you approach the session with the right mindset and achieve the correct, specific outcomes.

A recovery session is – as it sounds – about helping the body recover. Depending on how long you have been training, a recovery day may be a day off training, or it may simply be an easy swim, bike or run. The aim of a recovery session is to promote blood flow to the legs and aid in recovery. As such, it is completed at an easy Zone 1 to Zone 2 level and will be quite short.

The nature of the steady state set is more closely related to the long session, but is much shorter. These sets are all about adding additional volume or load to the program, and are conducted with a focus on Zone 2 training. Depending on your experience as a triathlete and the number of times you train per week, these sessions may or may not be present, as they're nowhere near as important as the sessions discussed above.

THE JUST-FOR-FUN SET

The 'just-for-fun' set is a term used at The Kona Journey to explain that you're going out for a training session purely to enjoy it. You may also hear triathletes talk about this sort of set as a 'coffee cruise' when completed on the bike. With the other sessions, you may be following different times, focus points and training objectives, and it can all become a bit much! You need to make sure you remember why you love triathlon, and regularly connect with the essence of being an Ironman triathlete and the reasons why you got into the sport. There is still a set time for this session, however, because without a time limit some triathletes would take this as a free ticket to swim, ride or run all day! But time is the only parameter; outside of that it's training for the freedom, enjoyment and love of being active.

You may be wondering at this point exactly what your training schedule is going to look like – how many training sets per week, how long your long sessions will be, how many interval sessions you need and so on. But don't worry, the point of the discussion here is to inform you about how to approach each type of training set. Later, in Chapter 11, we'll discuss training plans in more detail, and at the back of the book you'll find one fully spec'd training plan revealed in all its glorious detail. (Hmm, do I hear the sound of pages being turned?)

ₚ ⁴ᵇ ₚ ⁴ᵇ

You now have a clear understanding of the different training sets that can be used in the Ironman training program: the long session; intensity sets, including interval sets and fartlek sets; and tempo sessions. You have an appreciation of recovery sessions, steady state sets and just-for-fun sessions, and understand the aims and objectives of each. However, to fully come to grips with these sessions, in your body *and* mind, you are going to have to practise them. You won't be an 'expert' at these immediately; you will have to continue to practise and improve, and this may take many swim sets, bike rides and runs. But simply by going into a set with a goal and an objective that challenges you, you will be helping to progress your triathlon training and knowledge. There is no need to be overwhelmed; even if you are not yet there with your understanding of these sets, your fitness and understanding of your personal capabilities will already be improving, and that is fantastic.

The key take-away is that you have to get out there and swim, bike and run; experiment and try different sets, and challenge yourself! It will all start to come together. Whatever happens, remember, 'Just keep swimming, biking and running!'

CHAPTER 7

IRONMAN TECHNIQUES

Beyond the training sets discussed in the previous chapter, you also need to utilise specific long-distance training techniques to ensure that your training program is properly geared towards completing your best Ironman – giving you the best chance to qualify for Kona!

The Ironman techniques discussed here are all designed to build your strength as a triathlete, both physically and mentally, to ensure you are up for the challenge ahead. While these sessions will ensure that you have an Ironman body that's ready to race, they're also about developing confidence in your personal ability in each discipline; you will *know* that you're capable of both making the distance and swimming, biking and running well for the duration of the race. Make no mistake, it will take your best Ironman to get you to Kona!

The techniques that you utilise as an Ironman triathlete include, of course, techniques specific to the individual sports of swimming, cycling and running, but they also include techniques specific to triathlon and Ironman triathlon. These include double session days, brick sessions and race simulation training. You also need to ensure triathlon strength is in place. Yes, it's talked about a lot, but for an Ironman more than any other triathlon event, your swim, bike and run strength is essential to your success. To this end, you are going to become accustomed to hills and paddles. Hills, paddles, hills, hills, paddles, more hills and more paddles – you get the drift! You also need to do what you can to improve your cadence and get this to optimal levels for each discipline. And finally, you need to fully understand the interplay between the disciplines.

It's important to incorporate these Ironman techniques in your game plan because they're highly specific, but an additional benefit is that they make training more fun. You have variety across your plan, with many different focus points and challenges to engage you and help you progress. Lucky triathletes love variety!

These training sets are hard; they will challenge you, but that is all part of ensuring you're confident at the start of your race that you will make the finish line of your best Ironman. They also help to ensure your fitness improves at a quicker rate, but that's really just a bonus to all the fun you're going to have!

The usual risks apply if you choose not to follow these guidelines – DNFs and a lack of confidence, or indeed *no* confidence, at the start line. Now imagine you're at that start line– see that competitor standing next to you? If you follow these guidelines, you're bound to have more fun than they do on race day. You have included these techniques in your training and learnt the valuable lessons that they provide. And on we swim!

First we'll look in more detail at the different techniques involved in Ironman training, starting with techniques that are discipline specific.

SWIM TECHNIQUE

The first thing a triathlete needs to be keenly aware of when it comes to the swim leg of an Ironman triathlon is its challenging nature. A

3.8km open water swim is a far cry from a 1,500m pool swim. This means that we need to be aware of both the similarities and differences and take these into account.

First the similarities – both involve swimming freestyle. That's it. And now the important differences … one generally requires a wetsuit, the other doesn't. One is done in a highly controlled environment free of waves, currents, chop, wind, sighting and other swimmers bumping into you, and the other is not. One lasts about fifteen minutes, at which point the swimmer leaves the pool exhausted, and the other lasts from forty-five minutes to an hour and a half plus, at which point the swimmer enters transition and embarks on a 180km bike ride and a little marathon to finish. Quite frankly, the events and the training are nothing like each other, and so we need to prepare like a triathlete.

The right way to program swim sets will become apparent in the Ironman plan at the back of the book, but for now we'll go over some of the key points where your Ironman training will differ from regular swim training.

- Practise swim technique as part of your plan. If swimming is a challenge, invest in a swim coach who specialises in triathlon or open water swimming – the seconds you shave off your swim time through better technique make it worthwhile working on this in addition to your swim fitness. So do the hard work of improving your swim technique! However, don't focus on technique so much that you neglect developing your swim fitness. It's all about balance.

- Invest in a long set of fins to allow you to comfortably practise swim technique and improve both body position and propulsion. Just as you need to get aerodynamic on the bike, you need to get hydrodynamic in the pool.

- You should decrease the time you spend on kick sessions, as the kick only gives you a tiny amount (most experts put it at around 6-10%) of your propulsion. Dedicating a complete swim session to the kick is not an effective use of your time.

- Build up to and incorporate paddle and ultimately band work as part of your swim plan. Swim strength is vital for your 3.8km swim. Do this gradually – no injuries!

- Be smooth, efficient and relaxed when you swim and enjoy it.

We also need to ensure that the training sessions we do are longer in interval length than many pool-focused swim programs. Swimming only short, high intensity intervals is not going to prepare you for your 3.8km swim. That is, having a long break every 50, 100 or 200m (as you would do in a pool-based interval set when working towards a 50m, 100m, 200m, 400m and even 1500m swim event) is not what you do when training for a long bike or run, so why would this seem like a good idea when training for a long swim?

The other factor we need to talk about here is the mechanics of swimming. The fundamental premise of swimming is that you need to push directly back on the water in order to propel yourself forward; for every action there is an equal and opposite reaction – thank you Sir Isaac Newton! The more you push back on the water the faster you swim; this is your force output. Most swimmers need to work on their ability to exert a force on the water; this is the elusive 'feel for the water' swimmers talk about and why swimmers want to improve their catch. No arguments here!

However, what is often underestimated are the improvements that also need to be made to your stroke rate, or cadence. Force output and cadence are the two variables that will dictate your pace, or speed – a fact that applies across all three disciplines. In swimming, your cadence (stroke rate) is the number of times per minute your arm enters the water at the front of your stroke. In swimming, you should be aiming for a cadence of 55-60+. Many swimmers, especially open water swimmers (you are a triathlete and this makes you an open water swimmer, even though you may practice in a pool), need to improve their stroke rate. If your stroke rate is low it will be ineffective and inefficient when swimming in the open water. We need to ensure we have a punchy stroke with a stroke rate higher than many pool swimmers. This helps you combat the open water environment that you swim in and allows greater efficiency over longer distances.

Unfortunately, an in-depth look at open water swim technique is more than we can tackle in this book. If you need additional advice on open water swimming, then we suggest that you check out the work of Paul Newsome and Adam Young from Swim Smooth at www.swimsmooth.com. Paul is an absolute gun at open water swimming and has helped swimmers the world over to improve. Safe to say we are a big fan of his work. If you are ever fortunate enough to be in Perth, it's well worth heading along to a stroke correction session.

YOUR JOURNEY

1. Purchase a copy of Paul and Adam's book, *Swim Smooth – The complete coaching system for swimmers and triathletes,* and use it as a guide to improve your swim technique.

2. Read the profile descriptions or take the Swim Smooth quiz to determine what swim type you are. Use this as a basis to improve your swimming.

    www.swimtypes.com/your-type/

BIKE TECHNIQUE

Fortunately the bike is not as technique-driven as the swim and run. With this in mind, to help improve your bike technique we are going to suggest you head to the store and pay for a professional bike fit. Yes, they are expensive, but they are also necessary and, assuming you're an adult, once you've had one bike fit any subsequent fits become easier to do. This means it will be cheaper the next time you purchase a new bike and need it fitted. Naturally you need to have a bike fit from someone who understands triathlon, biomechanics and the body. There are a lot of rubbish bike fits going around and setting up a time trial bike is different from setting up a road bike – although we do suggest you get your road bike fitted at the same time.

Getting aerodynamic in a position that you can hold for 180km is also essential. Your torso is the biggest wind-blocking object on your bike and being aero will save you more time than that flash set of wheels. However, you also need to ensure that your position will not compromise your ability to run once you get off the bike. On your time trial bike one of the biggest areas of concern is ensuring a hip angle that is 'open'. Having a hip angle which is open is essential for you to be able to run successfully when you get off the bike; without it your stride length will suffer and this will decrease your run pace. (More about this shortly.) What this means is that you cannot simply go for the most aerodynamic position where your torso is against your top tube. You must balance your aerodynamic position with your hip angle and the flexibility you have in your body. Remember that you have a marathon to come after that bike ride, unlike the time trial stage of the Tour De France where they get a break when they finish. Repeat after me, 'I am a triathlete!'

Beyond bike fit and aerodynamics, the most important aspect of bike technique is to be smooth, efficient and relaxed while you ride. The aim on the bike is to exert force onto the pedals in a consistent, circular fashion. This means that you are pushing down on the pedals and pulling up on them as they go around. The biggest trick is to simply ensure you are not stomping on the pedals but are being smooth in your approach and exerting force in a circular fashion. As with the stroke rate in your swim, you also need to ensure that your cadence on the bike – the number of times that the pedals rotate per minute – is in the right zone to optimise your pace.

YOUR JOURNEY

1. Invest in a bike fit by someone who understands long-distance triathlon.

2. Focus on not bobbing in the saddle. Aim to be smooth, efficient and relaxed.

3. Check cadence is between 85 and 90.

RUN TECHNIQUE

As with the swim and bike, the aim on the run is to exert a force onto the ground that propels you forward. There will be force in both a vertical plane and a horizontal plane; however, the ultimate goal is to have as much force output in the horizontal plane as possible. In short, the more force output there is behind you in the horizontal plane, the faster you run. The best way to increase your stride length is with stronger muscles, which is done in your strength training, so we are going to dive into cadence here as this is a far easier way to improve your run efficiency. You should be aiming for 88+ strides per minute when running. To achieve this, you may need to decrease your stride length to be able to increase your cadence. Confused? Yes? Let me explain.

Your muscles work in a similar way to a rubber band. If a rubber band is just sitting there, minding its own business, there is no energy stored in it. However, if you stretch the rubber band, you can fling it across the room using its stored energy. When your running cadence hits the 88+ strides per minute range, your run efficiency improves because you are able to store some of the energy you have already generated and use it in your next stride.

YOUR JOURNEY

The best way to work towards an improvement in cadence is through small increments repeated regularly. A starting rate of 82 becomes 83, then 83 becomes 85, and you're pretty much there.

Cadence improvement is best tackled in small five-minute blocks on your easy recovery runs. For a five-minute period, focus on improving your cadence by two strides per minute before resuming your normal run. Repeat this two to three times throughout your recovery run. If you repeat this process on every recovery run, then the improved cadence will start to filter over into the entirety of your recovery run and your normal run. It takes a focused effort, but it does happen.

A word of caution, however. The above is based on flat terrain. As you run hills, your cadence will decrease relative to the gradient. It is important to try to keep cadence high. Therefore, it is important when selecting hills to run that you choose ones that still allow you to run rather than forcing you to walk because they're so steep.

STRENGTH EQUALS SPEED

While improving your technique across each discipline is vital, developing swim, bike and run strength is also essential if you want to do well in an Ironman. You need to be strong – very strong! An Ironman is long, and the back third of each discipline is all about strength.

Swim strength is all about paddles and, as you progress, the pull buoy and band, while bike and run strength is all about the hills and vertical gain. In triathlon, paddles and hills are the equivalent of lifting weights. Your body is the weight and your arms or legs have to complete many repetitions to propel you through the water or lift you up the hill. This provides a completely functional strength workout – it allows you to build the muscle fibres that are going to be needed if you want to complete your best Ironman.

We need to ensure that swim strength work is incorporated into the Ironman training program. This means that paddle work and the use of a pull buoy is included. As you progress this can become paddle and pull buoy work, and ultimately paddle, pull buoy and band. If this still doesn't create enough resistance for the elites, well, throw a sponge between your feet as well!

As I said, hills are the key when it comes to the bike. A hot tip for triathletes unable to get to hills easily for their bike session is to hit the wind trainer – it acts as a never-ending and unforgiving hill!

For the Ironman athlete, whenever possible, your fartlek and interval runs should be completed on rolling terrain or hills! You can often structure the workout by running towards the top of the hill and then turning and enjoying the run down. Such an approach has the effect of increasing the time spent running and has the fantastic benefit of using the hills to your advantage. You get a great workout on the way up the hill, and then, as your training progresses, you can use the downhills to your advantage as well by incorporating downhill efforts.

Hills are also the best way to build your long-distance speed. And this subject is important, because this is the area where many newbie Ironman athletes slip up. As discussed earlier, you may have come from a cycling or running background, which is fantastic, but completing a cycling road race or running 42km on fresh legs are very different experiences from what you will feel over the back part of the bike leg and final 12km of the run in an Ironman triathlon.

The critical point here is that your top-end speed in any discipline is *not* going to be your limiting factor when you complete your Ironman.

If you're not convinced, let's do a quick exercise. First, work out your approximate expected swim, bike and run time for your Ironman.

Be aware that to calculate your finish time you will have to add 10 minutes for transitions (hopefully this is more than enough).

When you've worked out your numbers you'll see that your average pace for each discipline is incredibly slow. Chances are you worked out those numbers twice because you thought you had made a mistake!

Race pace is surprisingly slow, and what this means with reference to the training program is that you don't need lots of fast reps; you need lots of longer distance reps at a lower speed. This is an Ironman triathlon, not a sprint-distance triathlon. These reps help build your muscular endurance. To intensify this, it helps if these longer reps can be completed uphill. The act of fighting gravity on each and every pedal or step intensifies the muscular endurance needed, so this type of workout simultaneously works the body's muscular and energy systems.

YOUR JOURNEY

Reflect on your current training and ask yourself:

- How many short intervals do you undertake?
- How often do you use paddles and pull buoy when you swim?
- How often do you ride the hills?
- How often do you run hills?

If you undertake lots of short intervals on large recoveries (i.e. 50 and 100m reps in the pool or flat 200, 400, 800m reps when running) we are quickly going to obliterate them from your training program and include longer intervals. If you have never used paddles, buy a pair! If you seldom bike in the hills, you are ideally going to increase that to once a week or more early in your program. And lastly, if you've not completed a run in the hills, building to complete at least one of your run sets in the hills will become your new aim.

DOUBLE SESSION DAYS

A double session day is when two sessions are completed on one day: one in the morning and one in the afternoon. Double session days can be in the same discipline or across disciplines, and are a great way to increase volume while lowering the risk of injury carried by completing a similar volume in a single session. When structured this way, the cumulative load across sessions needs to be taken into account.

The key point in this approach is that it allows for a recovery and re-fuelling period between sessions. Utilising this strategy often works at the midway point in a triathlete's training, when they're looking to step up the distance of their long session or are looking to add more volume to their program. They might need this strategy because they're new to triathlon, don't have large blocks of free time when they can schedule long sessions, or maybe they're looking to tackle a longer race – perhaps an Ironman. But the approach is valid for every triathlete, regardless of ability, as volume is relative to the individual. So, what does it look like in practice?

A mid-week double run could involve two shorter runs that collectively give you a significant total volume. This strategy also works brilliantly on the bike and swim, and it's a fantastic way to prepare your body for the demands of your Ironman. In any case, you need to look at the sets as a collective session, and be aware of the cumulative fatigue and effect that they will have on your body. You need to understand this *before* you begin a double session, because you need to allow enough energy in reserve to be able to complete the second session. This means you need to keep the first session in control, which involves sticking to the training plan and not overdoing things. Don't let the relative ease of a shorter first session trick you into pushing it. Trust me when I tell you that once the second session has been completed, you will be much more fatigued than you might expect. If you fail on this advice, you'll learn through experience with this one. After you have completed a couple of these types of sets, it becomes much easier to hold back on the first session – you know you need to be able to back up and swim, ride or run again later.

BRICK SESSIONS

There are two key skills that brick sessions aim to achieve: one is the ability to transition from the bike to the run and the second is the ability to run on tired legs. When you turn to the training program in the back of the book you'll see that we have included brick sessions, but perhaps not as many as you were expecting to see. This is because, while brick sessions have a place in the training program, they are often overdone by long-distance triathlon coaches.

While important to the Ironman triathlete, we must look at these with respect to the race. In a sprint- and Olympic-distance race, the transition and time allowed to settle into your bike or run pace is non-existent – these are pedal to the metal races from go to woe. On the other hand, in an Ironman you spend a lot more time biking and running, so you have time to settle into your groove. In fact it is very common for Ironman triathletes to go out of transition far too hard and destroy their race in the first 30km of the bike and first 10km of the run. Game over! As an Ironman athlete you need to be comfortable changing from one discipline to another, but this is less significant in these longer distance triathlons.

Other points to note are that Ironman triathletes generally have plenty of shorter distance race experience behind them, which means that they are comfortable with transitions and the effects these place on the body. Therefore these sessions should be used sparingly, which helps facilitate higher quality training within the ongoing program and ensure motivation remains high. Week after week of brick training after a long bike ride can become mentally taxing, as it detracts from the social nature of this session. Over time this can lead to a slip in quality and consistency with either the run or the bike, or indeed the entire set itself. The other option we have up our sleeves, of course, is to complete a short run in the afternoon after a long morning bike ride. Reduced injury risk and better quality training are two reasons we may look to such an approach.

You will also find that the programs often – but not always for the reasons discussed here – schedule the long run the day after the long bike or a bike set. This means that when you hit the long run you will still be fatigued, and therefore many of your long run sets will be completed on tired legs. There is no point in overdoing things and risking over-training by scheduling brick sets in a program that intrinsically mimics their effects.

Reduced injury risk and better quality training are achieved through keeping these longer brick sets for the final build into your race. This will give you confidence, but also ensure these sessions are exciting without being onerous. In this final part of your build into your best Ironman, you will be close enough to the race for motivation to be extremely high, which will ensure that your brick session is a quality training set. This in turn prevents it from feeling like just a 'regular' set that's become a drag. We don't want quality to suffer over the final part of your build, which is when it counts the most.

RACE SIMULATION

Race simulation occurs later in the Ironman plan. The focus of these sets is to more closely mimic the demands of race day. A race simulation gives you a chance to practise everything required for race day. This way, if and when things go wrong, you can implement changes to ensure that these problems do not occur on your big day. Race simulation days allow you to ensure everything is in order, especially your nutrition, race pacing and gear. You're also likely to face additional challenges in such a set that you would not normally have to deal with. Understanding how to overcome these problems and challenges gives you confidence that, when faced with similar issues in a race, you will know what to do and how to cope. You will be able to say, 'I have been here before and know how to deal with this situation.' This will give you the ability to overcome the challenge and move on – fast.

THE INTERPLAY BETWEEN THE DISCIPLINES

Finally, before we charge any further along, we must understand the interplay between disciplines. This is entirely unique to triathlon and multisport racing, but is exacerbated with Ironman triathlon due to the longer distances involved and the time spent in training.

The interplay between the disciplines means that we need to understand that if we complete one set, it can affect the next set or even several of the upcoming sets in your program. This could happen later that day, the following day or even later that week.

The most common way this presents itself is when you complete a hard training set in the morning and then go out and complete another training set in the afternoon. Unsurprisingly you may not have recovered completely from the morning set, and so you may find that you heart rate or effort is elevated in comparison to the speed or pace you feel you are training at. It is also common to experience this on a Sunday after a big day of training on the Saturday. If you ride on the Saturday and then go for a run on the Sunday, you may find your legs feel heavy and tired. Likewise if you run on the Saturday and then ride on the Sunday, you will often find your legs feel tired and take a while to warm up on the bike. This is certainly not a problem. This is the nature of triathlon training and racing. After all, you are going to have to complete a marathon after you have swum 3.8km and ridden 180km, so it's a safe bet that your legs are going to be a little tired at that stage! What is important is that we understand that this interplay happens and account for it in our training plan. Having a taper period built into the training program means that, come race day, the fatigue which presents itself will be manageable and something you can deal with.

•, •ㅇ •, •ㅇ

You now add to the mix an understanding of the specific long-distance training techniques that are used to train the Ironman triathlete. You understand key points around swim, bike and run technique. You appreciate that swim, bike and run strength are not only necessary, they are essential to completing your best Ironman, and you know how to go about building this strength. Finally, you've got your head around brick sessions and race simulation days and are aware of the importance of incorporating them into the overall plan, and can't wait to get started.

CHAPTER 8

PACING

Emma was excited as race day neared. She had all the usual nerves, but they were a good sign; they showed her that the race meant something. She knew she had done all of the hard work and had been training well for weeks. The race was in the bag! As she was treading water on the start line, waiting for the gun to go, she was quietly confident that she could have a great race; one that her kids and husband would be proud of, one that *she* would be proud of. This was it, she was going to qualify.

As the cannon went she started swimming. There was the sound of splashing all around, and she was swept up in the wave of excitement as all the triathletes charged off. She nailed her race start and found good feet, found her rhythm and settled in. Her race was unfolding beautifully. She exited the swim in a great position and moved smoothly through T1 and out onto the bike.

As kilometre upon kilometre drifted by, she felt great, lap one of the bike came and went as did lap two. This is how Ironman racing should be. Her nutrition was on song and hydration going well. She finished the bike and was delighted to exit T2 and hit the run.

Her watch hummed as the kilometres went by; she tried not to pay too much attention to the persistent shake on her wrist, but was delighted to know that she was well ahead of her goal time. She knew she was at the front of her age group and felt she could keep this up forever.

She kept running and savoured the moment. The course was spectacular, and as she ran past all her friends, family and club members she heard them cheering her on. They knew how hard she had worked for this and she could see how excited they were.

Then, almost suddenly, the feeling changed. What was happening? She had passed the 28km mark feeling great but now, just short of the 30km mark, her legs were failing! She had been feeling great until now. 'Why are they failing me?' Emma thought. But she tried to reassure herself, 'I have built up a buffer so it's not too bad, I'll still be able to make my goal time and I know I've got a lead on the others in my age group.'

To her dismay, her pace slowed and other runners started to pass her. She simply couldn't fight it; mentally she was giving it her all, but her pace just kept dropping. She started to walk and jog intermittently and struggled on, the finish line now in sight. When she finally crossed it, she slumped in a pile, exhausted and disappointed. She had done all of the training, she knew she was fit and she had been in front of her time and leading her age group! So what had happened?

What had happened was that her pacing was off. Pacing is one of the most under-valued skills in Ironman racing, yet it's essential for success at any level from age group triathletes right through to professional triathletes. You must have this skill if you want to make it to the finish line of your best Ironman and it will take your best Ironman to qualify for Hawaii! Working on and developing your pacing prowess can bring huge results, including personal bests and a much higher sense of satisfaction when you cross the finish line. You not only know you have swum, biked and run well, you also know that you have given it your all.

However, while a sound understanding of your personal pacing can deliver these results, pacing is not an improvement in fitness. It actually works with what you're already capable of doing. I love tapping into this latent potential with the Ironman athletes I work with. It delivers improved results without an improvement in fitness, but, as pacing knowledge increases, training sets improve and consequently fitness improves at a quicker rate as well. It's a win/win! And the best news? You can do it too!

So what is this elusive thing called pacing? Pacing is the ability to control your exertion over a period of time. To accept that pacing is important, we need to agree that the average pace per kilometre that you're capable of holding is quicker for a sprint-distance triathlon (750m/20km/5km) than a standard-distance triathlon (1500m/40km/10km). Similarly, the pace you can hold for a Half Ironman is quicker than it is for a full Ironman.

PACING AND THE BODY

As an Ironman triathlete you need a comprehensive understanding of pacing. This is the best way, physiologically, to deliver your personal best result. Let me put this in simple terms. Because of the way the body functions, two things happen if you overshoot in your event. First, you push your energy systems too far. This means that they need to have a period of recovery before you can return to a sustainable level. Second, you 'damage' your muscles. This is actually what you do when training, and is what helps you build strength – when the muscles recover, they come back stronger. However, this recovery takes days, and in a race you don't have time for this to happen.

Muscle damage equates to fatigue, so if you get your pacing wrong when racing, it equates to an exponential loss of time over the second half of your Ironman. To sum up, if you overshoot your energy systems, you need to back off to allow yourself to recover. If you overshoot for a prolonged period relative to your race distance in an Ironman, then you accumulate too much fatigue (muscle damage) early, and this causes you to slow exponentially over the reminder of the race.

You may have heard people talk about the famed negative split. This is when you run the second half of the race quicker than the first half of your race; this is relevant to each leg in a triathlon. And it's not all that hard to achieve if you go in with a pacing plan, as discussed below. If, however, you go in without a plan of action, then a negative split is exceedingly hard to achieve. Good pacing builds in a safeguard that allows you to have a great race every time. It gives you enough structure to put you in a position to have a great race, but also allows you the freedom to bike or run faster and exceed your goal when it counts.

HOW TO ACHIEVE PERSONAL PACING PROWESS

How many Ironman athletes have you heard say, 'My race was going great until the run' or 'I was flying until I hit the 30km mark of the run?' Of course things didn't go wrong earlier – if they had you'd have been too embarrassed to admit it and, quite frankly, if that was the case you weren't even in the ball park of getting your race right. These comments are a sign that you need to work on your ability to pace yourself throughout your race. The fact is, a great run is set up on the bike. While time-wise the run is shorter than the bike, you need to be able to run well off the bike if you are going to qualify for Kona.

So how do you go about achieving the famous negative split? There are two things you need to do:

1. Practise pacing in training.
2. Have a pacing plan when you race.

We're going to look at pacing your race before we talk about practising pacing in training, because it's easier to come to grips with this subject in the context of a race. The key to the pacing plan is to break each leg of your race into thirds, or nearly thirds, with the exception of the swim. We are going to work backwards through the race because the concept is easiest to understand with regard to the run, then we'll apply it to the bike and finally we'll tackle the swim.

PACING THE RUN

So, what this 'chunking' looks like for a **MARATHON** is a 15km chunk, a second 15km chunk and a final 12km chunk. Your aim is to run the first 15km at goal-race pace plus five seconds per kilometre. For the middle chunk, you drop your pace down to goal-race pace. Then for the final chunk, you bring it home with everything that you have left, ideally goal-race pace less five or more seconds per kilometre.

You might be doing the maths and thinking, 'This means I'm going to be 15 seconds off my goal pace.' In a strict sense this is the case; however, this strategy has the potential to allow you to exceed, if not obliterate, your Ironman run PB. Chances are that over the final 12km, you're going to be feeling great and will be more than five seconds per kilometre under your race pace. If you're not, then your aim is just to hold your expected race pace through to the finish, which still allows you to have a fantastic race based on what you are truly capable of.

Interestingly, this means that you should hit the 30km mark feeling great (well, as great as you can, having just banked 3.8, 180 and 30km at a steady clip). When everyone else hits struggle town you'll be in your groove, hitting the afterburners and flying for home. Watch as you pass all those people who had a poor pacing strategy. Winning ... and claiming your ticket to Kona!

We also suggest here that you pay particular attention to the first 1-8km of your run. Having thrown the bike away after 180km you will be glad to be out the saddle and be hit with a great shot of adrenalin as you enter the final leg. This causes most people to charge out of T2 like superman or superwoman. They bank the first kilometre in record time, thinking, 'Wow I'm on today.' Feeling great, they try to hold this pace, despite all their training telling them otherwise, only to be left walking by the 21km mark. If we are aware that this is going to happen we can put a strategy in place to ensure we know what to do and are left flying at the right point in the race – the final 12km.

The strategy we recommend is to be aware that you are likely to run your first kilometre faster than your goal pace. Be aware of this and try to hold back slightly. If you do run too fast, then you need to, in fact you MUST, bring this back to your goal pace over the next 1-2km. Failure to have slowed to your goal pace by the third kilometre of the run is GAME OVER!

Assuming that you have now kept your pace in control for the first 3km, it is recommended that you build into your run over the first 8km, by which stage you should have settled into your goal-race pace. This gives your body time to transition from the seated position on the bike (condensing your hip flexors) to the tall standing position of the run. Your hip flexors are directly related to your stride length and thus your pace. Give them time to stretch out and move freely; there are plenty of kilometres coming up when you can run faster. So, in short, if you are slow over the first 8km, fantastic. You have set your run up beautifully.

Note that you can also use your RPE to check you're running at the right speed at the right time and therefore pacing yourself properly. You should feel in control for the first section, steady for the second section, and run hard in the final section. This is where RPE becomes vital, and why practising pacing in training is important – it teaches you how to know and understand what your goal intensity 'feels' like.

As fatigue builds, you may find that you're only capable of holding your initial easy pace, but suddenly that feels a lot harder. Fatigue is going to happen to everyone, so what you have to do is prevent these fatigue levels rising too quickly. If fatigue levels rise too quickly, you may find that you don't make it to the finish or are left having to slow your running drastically or even walk.

A pacing plan accepts that fatigue is going to occur but keeps you in a great position by preventing it from rising too quickly, allowing you the freedom to run faster when it counts. Patience, patience, patience.

PACING ON THE BIKE

Now that we understand the concept of pacing, it is easy to replicate for the bike. Break things into three 60km chunks. If you have a power meter, great; you can use this to guide your effort. If, however, you only have speed, then you are going to have to use your heart rate and RPE to determine the right pace. As with the run, on the bike you need to keep the first section in control, stay steady for the second and, unlike the run, also say steady for the third. Obviously, you have a marathon to come! As with the run, don't necessarily expect your speed/power to increase over each segment, but as fatigue builds you will find sustaining the same effort suddenly feels a lot harder.

Lastly, for the bike as for the run, build into things over the first 5-10km. Your body is in the process of diverting blood from the shoulders to the legs. This takes time. Don't dilly-dally, but be sensible.

PACING THE SWIM

Now to the swim. The swim is, well... a different kettle of fish.[20] This is because, in this leg, you are allowed to draft. Drafting is the easiest way to save energy and produce a swim time far faster that you can achieve on your own. Drafting makes a profound difference to your time because water is so thick. So instead of chunking your time and adjusting your pace accordingly, the pacing plan for your swim leg is more about knowing how to draft properly.

The fast swimmers are going to go hard off the start line – they are chasing the open water. This means that if you are going to be able to draft off the feet of a faster swimmer, you are also going to have to move quickly off the start line and be able to start your swim quicker than other swimmers of a similar ability. That is, you have to be the swimmer who gets on the feet of a faster swimmer rather than being the faster swimmer who is 'towing' a slower swimmer around the

20   How could I resist a pun like that!

course. In reality this is about having a quick 25-50m sprint and being prepared to cover the first 25-100m (30 to 60 seconds) at a speed in excess of what you plan to swim at. The trick is to go much quicker, but not at an all-out sprint.

After this time you need to find the feet, let the initial fatigue pass and settle into what should be a steady effort. In the swim everything is done on feel, and there is no looking at your watch or knowing exactly how far you have been. After you have found the feet stick with them through to the end of the swim, sighting as you need and finding new feet at the turn buoys if needed. Oh, and don't tap the feet! This is insanely annoying to the swimmer in front who is doing the hard work of towing your arse around the course. If you do this, expect them to swim to drop you or even get a foot to the face!

PACING YOUR IRONMAN USING ZONES

Now we're going to refine your understanding of pacing further by applying the concept of training zones to pacing. Because it's too hard to look at your watch when swimming or know exactly how far you've swum, it's difficult to correctly identify your zones, but you can certainly use them to help you pace the bike and run. Think back to Chapter 3 and what you learnt about intensity and zones. Remember that combining heart rate, RPE and pace/power gives you the best guide to your intensity, and the level of intensity that you identify correlates to a particular zone. When this knowledge is combined with an understanding that fatigue builds over the entirety of a race, it places you in a position to ensure you nail the critical element of pacing. As discussed, you need to break your race up into thirds or skewed thirds of 60/60/60 or 15/15/12, and then ensure you're in the right zone at the right time. But remember that the exact feel and intensity that you're capable of holding is unique to each triathlete and must be practised in training – ideal pacing won't just happen.

As a guide, for the bike portion of your Ironman, you need to operate in Zone 2 and be wary of allowing your heart rate to drift into Zone 3, even on the hills. To clarify, if you're expecting a finish time *under* 10 hours you will be at the upper end of Zone 2, if you are aiming for around 12 hours, then aim for Zone 2; if you're expecting a finish time *over* 12 hours, aim to keep it in Zone 1 and low Zone 2. For the bike, aim to keep your heart rate consistent at these levels; however, you can expect the effort required to maintain this level to increase dramatically.

This leaves you with the run to go. On the run it's no different – if you're expecting a finish time *under* 10 hours you will be at the upper end of Zone 2; if you're aiming for around 12 hours, then aim for Zone 2; if you're expecting a finish time *over* 12 hours, aim to keep it in Zone 1 and low Zone 2. Over the final 12 km of the run you can either look to maintain this pattern through to the end or, if you feel you have gas left in the tank, you can look to increase your effort over the final segment. By this stage, you will be able to make an educated and informed decision about what you're capable of. You will increase your pace when it counts, and pass all those who went out too hard at the start and had a poor pacing strategy. Even though you'll be in the hurt locker, imagine how great you're going to feel as you pass all those people!

YOUR JOURNEY

While you now have a pacing plan in place, good pace control won't just happen come race day. You need to practise it in training. You can practise pace control in almost any set, and below are a few examples. Always complete an appropriate warm-up before a set, and a suitable cool down afterwards.

For a short pacing set, complete the following set on the bike or run. Divide the set into three 10-minute blocks or, on the bike, three 10km blocks – 10/10/10 – and pace yourself as follows:

- Block 1 – race pace plus 5 seconds per km
- Block 2 – goal-race pace
- Block 3 – race pace less 5 seconds per km.

Complete the 10/10/10 segments straight through, programming them into your watch or hitting the lap key between sections. This mimics what you will undertake on race day when your blocks would be 15km, 15km and 12km, or 60km chunks on the bike.

For a longer pacing set complete the following using the same concept, but move the blocks out to 15 minutes/km or even 20 minutes/km. So the set becomes 15/15/15 or 20/20/20. Pace yourself as follows:

- Block 1 – goal marathon pace less 5 seconds per km or slightly slower than goal bike RPE/ power.

- Block 2 – goal marathon or bike pace.

- Block 3 – goal marathon pace less 5 seconds per km or slightly quicker than goal bike RPE/ power.

Complete the 15/15/15 or 20/20/20 segments straight through, programming them into your watch or hitting the lap key between sections.

To mix things up further, in the shorter set you could aim to hold your Half Ironman/70.3 pace while the longer set could be completed at Ironman race pace. Make sure to complete the set on terrain similar to your target race. In other words, if your race includes hills or undulations, complete the set on similar terrain. If you course is flat, complete the set on terrain that mirrors your course.

While the above examples provide great ways to practise pacing in higher intensity training sets, the following set is something that we recommend you undertake on a ride or run as your Ironman nears to help your prepare for your race.

Divide your set into three 40-minute blocks – 40/40/40 – and pace yourself as follows:[21]

- Block 1 – easy

- Block 2 – steady

- Block 3 – hard (But don't go over the top, as this is a two-hour set, and when you tackle your Ironman you will be running and biking for much longer than this. If you start to feel the signs of fatigue after two hours, consider how that would play out exponentially over another six, seven, eight or more.)

---

21   Keep in mind that this is a long set and, depending on where your personal running or cycling is currently at, you may need to build up to this.

With this set, we recommend completing a 60-second walk or spin between sections. Aim to keep the 60-second walk or spin separate from the 40-minute blocks. This allows you to compare the average pace, speed (depending on wind) or power achieved in each block without it being skewed by the 60-second recovery. Keep in mind that a change in terrain, road surface or hills can, and likely will, affect your average pace or speed for each segment. One way to combat this is to complete segments over the same course, such as three mini loops.

As you get closer to your race, you can gradually increase the length of the 40-minute segments to one hour, although we would only recommend doing this on the bike. This will create a continuing challenge and begin to more accurately match the demands of race day, both in terms of the time and the energy demands required. This set would look like this:

- 60 minutes, easy
- 60 minutes, steady
- 60 minutes, hard.

Completing one-hour loops over the same course is a fantastic way to determine your pacing control and start to fully appreciate the effects of fatigue on the body. At the conclusion of the set, compare the average heart rate and speed/power for each segment. Comparing your first lap to your last lap often provides the most interesting comparison. Correlating the data with how you *feel* or *felt* can provide the best insight about your personal pacing. From this point, you can refine and practise your pacing in subsequent training sets.

You are now equipped with the knowledge required to improve your race pacing and your pacing in training. If you find it difficult at first, don't worry, that just demonstrates that you have more to gain than someone who nails it the first time. Don't be disheartened and stick with it – it just takes practice. And that just means more biking and running, which certainly can't be a bad thing, right?

The two things you are going to commit to are:

1. Practising a pacing set at least once in your training. Make sure you review your data afterwards to see how you went.

2. Leading into your next race, you are going to go in with a pacing plan as outlined above, following the rule of thirds. Try it at least once; you will be surprised at what you're capable of!

⠄⠂ ⠄⠂ ⠄⠂ ⠄⠂

You now have a firm understanding that pacing in an essential technique that requires mastery by the Ironman athlete. You understand that you can push both your energy systems and your fatigue level too far and too early in a training set or race. This is detrimental to your overall goal, as it can cause you to exponentially slow over the final part of your race. You understand that to combat this you need to hit a negative split. Having a pacing plan that you can implement will ensure this occurs. You're also aware that this won't just happen by magic, but that you need to practise this in training. You need to undertake a range of training sets so that you can practise and refine your pacing to ensure that you master it. Knowledge and understanding is one thing, but implementation is another, so you best get out there training. Next, in Part 3, we bring everything together and develop your body into a long-distance weapon!

PERFECT PREPARATION

Imagine having your perfect Ironman.

You start the swim with purpose. You fly off the line, find feet and then sit in for an easy swim. It's effortless and you hit the bike feeling great.

On the bike the uphills are swift, the downhills enjoyable. You're peddling smoothly as the winding road disappears beneath your wheels. You're in the zone and the kilometres are sailing by. You're thinking, 'Wow, it's great to be out riding.'

Your through T2 and out onto the run. You have never felt so great leaving T2. It's incredible. On the run the kilometres drift by. Everything is going perfectly: you're floating, you're fast, you're in the moment and you're on your way to punching your ticket to the Big Island!

Now let's take it a bit further. You've finished the race and achieved a long-cherished dream. What is that dream? Maybe it was to finish with an Ironman PB, maybe it was to hit the top ten in your age group or make the podium. Maybe it was to visit the roll down, not waiting for a roll down but knowing you have claimed your spot to Hawaii. Regardless of what that dream was, triathlon is a lifestyle choice and you're going to be back for more!

But making it to Kona doesn't have to be just a dream. If you make your dream a goal, you have the power to make it come true by focusing on what you do between now and that perfect race. You are capable of achieving your dream; and this, the final part of this book, will show you how to do that!

Of course, there is no guarantee that you will get everything perfect the first time, and every time. You will make mistakes. That's no problem at all – that's called learning and it's all part of the journey. But if you give it a go, the worst thing that can happen is that you will improve, and that's certainly not a bad thing.

One good training set won't improve your fitness. One good week of training will do little to improve your fitness. There is no magical set. It's consistent commitment to your Ironman training program, over a prolonged period of time, that will deliver results. Long-term consistency is the cornerstone, but it's also vital that you do the right 'work' as it relates to your end goal.

This section is where all the knowledge you have been exposed to comes together. The first part of preparing for your race is about gathering your team. Then, after understanding some key principles, we'll get to the hardcore stuff. You will see how an Ironman training program is structured; this includes the short, middle and long-term plans. You will see how and why a taper is needed, and how, often overlooked, recovery is included within an Ironman training program. Finally you will tackle your big dance, your big day: race day. You will have concerns but they will be covered in detail. The questions that you may not have thought about yet, the ones that come up at the last minute, will be covered. No stone will be left unturned. You will finish this book confident that when you front the start line for your Ironman, you will be prepared, will make the finish line and have your best race yet.

CHAPTER 9

GATHER YOUR TEAM

When embarking upon the journey of training for your best Ironman, you need to be aware that while the final effort may be a solo endeavour, there is a team of people behind the scenes who play vital roles in enabling you to stand at the start line and feel confident about the task ahead.

Without this team in place you face an increased risk of injury, and are in danger of using your training time poorly and missing training sets. You might find yourself with a body that is beat up and a life that's out of balance. People often look to the 'pros' and think, 'But they're able to achieve this all on their own!' Not true. The pros use a team better than anyone. Take Olympic great James Tomkins, for example, who is a multiple Olympic gold medallist, has won medals at four consecutive Olympic Games and has been Australian Olympic team captain – and that's just scratching the surface of his achievements! He has a coach, mentors, a physiotherapist and a massage therapist on his team, and he also has a supportive family. Sure, they may not be paraded front and centre and may not get a mention in public, but they are there behind the scenes doing their jobs. Every elite-level football team also has support staff on hand as does every elite triathlete, even if their team behind the scenes is not mentioned. Why? Because it enhances the individual's, and consequently the team's, chance of success.

Having a team in place makes the journey more rewarding and allows you to achieve your impossible dream, the one that finishes where Ironman began.

With a little bit of knowledge, it's not hard for you to implement the same approach that professionals use and watch your ability to achieve your best Ironman skyrocket. How we go about achieving this is through working with independent providers, each of whom specialise in one area. So let's discuss the people on your team, why you need them and how to ensure they're playing a pivotal role in your race preparation.

THE SUPPORTIVE FAMILY – YOUR CLOSEST ALLY

The first group you need on your side is your family. This is especially important if there are dependent kids involved, or if you plan on completing more than one Ironman, which you are clearly going to have to do! You need to include these critical people in your journey. If they're not involved, they may end up resenting your training and feel that it detracts from the family-life balance – they'll think your triathlon is taking you away from them. If the family feels this way about your training, they may push back against you and your beloved sport. This resentment can cause your family to make training more challenging than it already is, and can make you feel alone in your endeavour. You certainly don't want that. However, if you take a few steps to involve your family in your journey, they can become an active part of it. They will enjoy what your training brings to family life, and encourage and support you more than you ever anticipated.

So how do you go about ensuring that your family supports you? You need to involve them. They need to feel a part of the journey towards your achievement, but without finding their role onerous. Each family and their individual life and work commitments are different, but there are many and varied ways to involve the family in your Ironman journey – especially your training. The following list provides a starting point:

- If you're running on the road, choose paths that are appropriate for bikes so the kids can ride with you. As they get older, they will be able to outride you. They can also be great water carriers.

- Mix your training up once in a while so that your big ride or run day doesn't fall on the weekend. This can be achieved in a number of ways, such as double bike or run days. This gives you more time with the family on the weekend; something they will thank you for.

- If you always bike or run in the morning, change it to an afternoon session once a month so that you're around in the morning and can spend time with the kids or your partner.

- Organise for the family to meet you for coffee after your swim, bike or run. This can be a great way to complete an open water swim and treat the kids to a trip to the beach or lake at the same time. Or you can bike or run point-to-point rather than in a looped or out and back course, as you conveniently now have a lift back.

- Let the kids know that training is something that is really important for you, but ask them if there's something special they would like to do when you've finished, such as playing mini golf, going to a movie, playing at the beach or visiting a new park. Make sure you keep your promise and treat them to the outing they want when you're back from your swim, bike or run. This helps kids to associate your training with quality, fun family time.

- Encourage your partner to swim, ride or run. If they're new to training, they may have to come on one of your easy sessions, or alternatively aim to finish at the same time and place for coffee.

- Make a weekend of it and have a family getaway. This allows you to find new pools to swim in, roads to ride on and paths or trails to explore on your run.

People regularly underestimate the importance of having the family on side with their training, but by involving them in your journey it increases the enjoyment and fun for all. And the best bit? Swimming, biking and running is screen free, quality family fun!

YOUR JOURNEY

Over the next two weeks, make sure to include your partner or kids in your training at least once. Make sure to unlock the fun and feel the meaning that triathlon brings to your lives.

Now let's discuss the professionals you need.

THE IRONMAN COACH – FAST-TRACKING YOUR SUCCESS

The first professional to put into your corner is a coach – someone who has been there before and understands how to guide you on your journey. This is important, as this guidance will allow you to invest your training time where it's most beneficial. Through their knowledge and expertise, a coach is able to guide you to achieving your desired results more quickly. This allows you to unlock goals you never before thought possible. An informal survey run by Training Peaks found the top seven reasons athletes liked to work with a coach were: accountability, structure, smarts, reduced risk of over-training, motivation, time management, and finally but importantly, so 'they don't have to do the thinking'.[22] Collectively, these factors combine to give triathletes who are coached greater improvement, and increased improvement rates, than those who aren't. Moreover, there are risks if you don't put a coach in your corner. These include DNFs, DNSs, injuries, dwindling motivation and a failure to see the big picture about what you're trying to achieve. In short, without a coach a triathlete who is capable of qualifying for Kona may simply never achieve the dream because they haven't implemented the best training for them and have never raced to their full potential – their best Ironman.

But despite the obvious benefits of working with a coach, Ironman triathletes often find that taking this step takes them out of their comfort zone. Regular comments include:

- I'm fearful of commitment.
- I'm not good enough!

22   https://www.trainingpeaks.com/blog/the-top-7-reasons-to-work-with-a-coach/

- No one would want to work with me!

- I'm just not comfortable working with a coach.

- It wouldn't benefit me.

These are all excuses used to avoid the uncomfortable feeling of taking that first step and contacting a coach. However, it's often the triathletes who are most reluctant to work with a coach who, after finally taking the plunge, can't imagine Ironman training without one. They love being coached by a professional and the benefits it brings.

CHOOSING A COACH

There are three ways that you can take action in this important area. The first is to find a local or online Ironman coach, and I highly recommended this. Whether it's joining my community at The Kona Journey or engaging another local or online Ironman coach, there are three essentials to look for before you employ someone:

1. You have to believe in their coaching philosophy.

2. They need to believe in you as the athlete.

3. The coach-athlete relationship has to gel so that you can function as a team.

This is likely to seem pretty straightforward, and it is, except when it doesn't work.

At this point it's important that I share a story from my past. Since being a younger athlete and through to today, I have had many coaches (I believe it's important for everyone to receive professional coaching, even a coach). I once had an exceptional coach, whom I decided to work with so he could help me achieve my endurance goals. Although his coaching philosophy was on song with mine, I enjoyed his training sets and he believed in me as an athlete, we just didn't gel. Needless to say, a few months later we both went our separate ways. One of the three essential ingredients was missing: we simply couldn't function as a unit.

Sometimes this lack of cohesion will be apparent immediately, in which case you should walk away immediately. Other times this lack of cohesion will not be immediately apparent, as was the case for me. After making contact with a coach and finding your initial conversations all go well, you'll find that the athlete-coach relationship will still take time to build. Over the first four to eight weeks the coach is learning about how you function as a triathlete, and you're learning about how the coach likes to operate. If the coach-athlete relationship doesn't feel right after this time, don't be afraid to, politely, walk away and find another coach.

I will be the first to say that I am not the perfect coach for every Ironman athlete, nor am I going to enjoy working with every triathlete. No coach is right for every athlete and no athlete is right for every coach. I'll also let you in on a secret here – if it's not working for you, it's not working for your coach! I am proactive in this matter, but not all coaches are, so don't be afraid to cut the ties if it's not working and make sure you find a perfect match.

If the cost of hiring a professional Ironman coach is prohibitive, then your next option is to find an Ironman triathlon mentor. Someone you know and trust, and who has achieved goals similar to yours.

Much like a coach, they can provide a unique perspective. Other triathletes are normally more than happy to pass on their knowledge, and they also make great training partners. Do be careful, however, to select the 'right' mentor. While you may think you can find one among your best friends, and find someone who means well, there is a lot of misinformation out there and you could be putting your trust in someone who's not really keen or up to the job. So make sure their apparent knowledge really is what it's reputed to be by asking about their experience. And don't think your friends will be offended if you look outside your immediate circle for a mentor –sometimes this is the best way to find a mentor with the appropriate perspective on your situation.

Lacking someone who might be a suitable mentor, the final option you have is to join a local triathlon group or triathlon club. The regularity and structure provided by training with a group is great, as it yields a huge source of motivation and allows you to meet like-minded individuals. But a word of warning! Be careful with the triathlon group you select, as Ironman triathlon is different from sprint- or standard-distance triathlon. In the past I have seen triathletes join triathlon groups not well suited to their goals.

We want you to be open to the idea of hiring an Ironman coach or working with an Ironman coaching program, but today we are simply planting a seed and opening your mind to the possibilities of fast-tracking your progress. After you have finished reading this book, you will be in a more powerful position to know what you are after when it comes to an Ironman coach.

THE PHYSIOTHERAPIST – PREVENTION, NOT CURE!

The next person you need in your team is the physiotherapist.[23] This person is essential to your team. Now, you might be thinking, 'But I'm not going to get injured!' But I don't want you to think cure, I want you to think prevention and improved performance. The first time you see your physiotherapist should be *before* you start training or, more likely in your case, before increasing your training load. Why? Let me explain.

You need to understand what is often referred to as the 'injury window'. This period occurs three to four weeks after you start training, increase your training load, or return from injury or illness. The body can absorb the increased load easily enough for a while, but suddenly, at this three to four-week mark – boom! Your body finally breaks. This can occur for a number of reasons, but the most common are:

- Increasing the swim, bike or more commonly run load too quickly (this can be how much or how fast you're swimming, biking and running each week as a whole, or within any discipline).

- A muscle imbalance.

- A limited range of motion.

When injury strikes, all that motivation you had and all that fitness you put in place is gone in an instant. But if we take the prevention course, we anticipate potential injury and put steps in place to ensure it doesn't occur.

---

23 Some people prefer the chiropractor, osteopath, etc. For this book I am not going to enter that debate, I am going to go with physiotherapist, but you may choose your appropriate professional.

This simply means two things: a structured approach to increasing your training load, and booking in to see your local physiotherapist for an exercise pre-screen. Your physiotherapist will be able to tell if you're fundamentally weak in any particular area, or if you have a limited range of motion that needs to be rectified. They will give you the guidance to solve the problem and get you on your way.

Stan Garland, an Ironman triathlete, Hawaii Ironman finisher and physio guru who has worked around the world, assisted Olympians and elite athletes from numerous sporting codes and worked with weekend warriors as well as countless triathletes, states that:

An exercise pre-screen has the ability to not only decrease your chances of injury but also increase your performance, as you are now able to recruit the appropriate muscles required for efficient training.

The other time your physiotherapist is going to be your best friend is when you get a 'niggle'. There is a difference between 'sore from training', a.k.a. fatigue, and 'injury pain'. Learning this difference is important. If and when you recognise any potential injury signs, be proactive rather than reactive – book yourself in for an appointment. It's tough for triathletes to accept, but a few days off training now is better than three months off later – just think about how grumpy you would be about the latter! Plus, chances are it's only going to be time off one discipline, which can allow you to sensibly focus some additional time on another aspect, such as swim technique.

Stan recommends booking in to see a physio if any of the following signs are present:

- Niggles that are persistent, i.e. three days plus. Any longer than a week and you risk interrupting your long-term consistency.

- Unusually sore muscles.

- Sharp pains.

CHOOSING A PHYSIO

If you don't have a physiotherapist, I would encourage you to ask the following questions or search for the following information before enlisting their services. If you already have a physiotherapist, mentally check that they tick these boxes:

- Can three triathletes (preferably more) recommend their services and results?

- Do they have a personal interest in triathlon?

The second point is essential. Time and time again triathletes start with a 'generic' physiotherapist, who doesn't truly appreciate what they do – even in sports physiotherapy circles completing an Ironman is not considered normal! You need someone on your team who understands the unique needs of long-distance endurance sports, specifically Ironman triathlon, as well as uniquely understands the demands of swimming, biking and running.

YOUR JOURNEY

Ask around your local triathlon circles and find a physiotherapist who works with triathletes. Book in and organise an athletic pre-screen to help identify problems that may come up as you increase your training. Then take the steps outlined by the physiotherapist to prevent these problems from occurring. If you walk away from your appointment with no concerns, this is fantastic – you can feel even more confident about what you're about to tackle!

THE REMEDIAL MASSAGE THERAPIST

A car needs a service, and so do your muscles. The final professional to put in your team is the remedial massage therapist. I'm not talking the light fluffy stuff here, I'm talking about a deep tissue massage that provides relief for muscles that have been working hard. The training you will be undertaking on a weekly basis means that regular massage is imperative to keeping you free of injury and swimming, biking and running freely.

According to remedial massage therapist Michael Fildes, who has worked with the likes of Rohan Dennis (Tour de France stage winner and Olympic medallist) and Jenni Screen (Olympic basketball champion), as well as elite Australian Rules footballers:

The benefits of massage are outstanding. When someone hops on the table for a massage I can always tell by the feel of their muscles if they have regular massage or not; the difference is quite astounding. When you are exercising you are causing your muscles and the surrounding tissues to tighten up. By having a deep tissue massage we can help to break up the toxins and elements that have accumulated that make you feel tighter.

Ideally, Ironman triathletes should be getting a massage every one to two weeks, but this is not possible for many. However, it's recommended that you book in at least every three to four weeks for a remedial massage. The volume of training that you're tackling means that you need to keep on top of things rather than let problems develop, which makes it much harder to solve them.

CHOOSING A MASSAGE THERAPIST

Finding a good remedial massage therapist can be difficult. Michael suggests triathletes use the following questions to find out if the massage therapist will be good value. If they don't provide a great deep tissue massage, don't be afraid to move on until you find one who does.

- Can you describe to me the type of massage technique you use and how you physically work on clients?

- What other sports people do you work on and what type of sport do they participate in?

- What benefits can I expect as a result of your remedial massage?

- How regularly do you perform deep tissue massage?

YOUR JOURNEY

This one is easy. Find an appropriate remedial massage therapist and book an appointment within the next fortnight – no cancelling! While you may not completely enjoy the massage, you will enjoy the results.

THE DOCTOR – GET A MEDICAL PRE-SCREEN

While they do not form part of your ongoing team, visiting your regular doctor for a medical pre-screen is always recommended prior to undertaking a specific Ironman training program.

Now you know the team that you need around you to increase your chances of success on your Kona journey. You know who you need on your team and why each of these people is essential. You understand that elite-level athletes, and sporting teams, have these professionals in place to help ensure their success, and so must you.

To recap, your team members are:

- The supportive family – your closest ally

- The Ironman coach – fast-tracking your success

- The physiotherapist – prevention, not cure

- The remedial massage therapist – a car needs servicing, so do your muscles.

You need to be proactive in putting each of these helpers in place. You want not just a good team, but a great team. Their support will become increasingly important as you progress on your Ironman journey.

CHAPTER 10

UNDERSTANDING PLANNING

Now that you've got your support team in place, I bet you're dying to lock in a training plan and start working it. But you need to be patient for just a little longer. Everything that follows will make better sense if you understand some of the principles behind an Ironman training plan, and you need to do this before you hit the water, jump on your bike or lace up your shoes. It always helps to know why you should do something, and why you should do it in a particular way, before you set out on the journey of learning how to do it.

PLANNING – YOUR SECRET WEAPON

Imagine you're setting off on an overseas trip, and have just got off the plane in a city you have never been to before. You've heard about a divine local waterfall with hot springs at the bottom of it. It's hidden in thick jungle and difficult to get to, but you're determined to set out on the journey to find it. What's the first thing you do after you've got through immigration and had your passport stamped? Do you just start walking and hope to stumble across it? Unlikely. You're more likely to ask someone who has been there before to guide your journey. They'll be able to tell you about any obstacles to expect and the provisions you'll need along the way – maybe you'll need to camp out, maybe you'll need food. Your advisor might even be able to draw a map for you. With this help, you'll understand the journey ahead and what you need in terms of both your skill set and your knowledge. Sure, you can set off armed with nothing, and hope that you'll get lucky and stumble across the waterfall, but chances are it will take you a lot longer than if you'd first sought the guidance of someone who has been there before.

In this case, your divine waterfall is the finish chute of your best Ironman. To get there, you're going to have to go on a journey. Not just a journey on race day, but a journey that starts with the preparation and planning necessary to ensure you are successful.

Having a plan in place is beneficial because it provides guidance and structure, helping to prevent you from becoming overwhelmed by the task at hand. Without a plan, you're leaving things up to chance. You can run out of time to refine and improve elements of your Ironman triathlon in your training, or even forget to work on whole elements. This leaves you feeling underprepared a few weeks out from your race, and that's certainly not the frame of mind you want to have when you hit the start line.

Another benefit of having a specific plan in place is the focus, clarity and direction it brings to your training. As the saying goes, 'How do you eat an elephant? One bite at a time.' Ironman training is no different. The Ironman plan allows you to focus on the critical things that you need to complete each and every day (unless, of course, it's a day off) in order for you to reach your Kona dream. This focus allows your mind to be at ease, as you know that over time all the required boxes of training and race preparation will be ticked. All you need to do is put your best effort into following the plan and what is prescribed in each session. Simple, right?

CONSISTENCY

No single training set, on its own, will deliver the improvements you're after. It is groups of training sets, blocks of training and long-term consistency that deliver results. A training plan is a vital component for ensuring that long-term consistency, and has a knack of ensuring your commitment. Often triathletes don't realise the importance or effect of a training plan until they have actually been on one. Once they *have* been on one, they're unlikely to go without one again. The training plan allows habits to be built and cemented into place. It enables you to start slowly and develop consistent training before progressing to the next step and building on your progress. These habits become routine and, before you know it, your fitness and skill level has shifted exponentially – and you have only just got started!

Beyond having a plan, great triathletes use a few other tricks to help them maintain long-term consistency. And while it sounds simple, one of these tricks is to keep a training diary. You have two options for this: pen and paper or an online program. Online options include programs such as Training Peaks (The Kona Journey's go-to option), Strava (affectionately known as Facebook for athletes) or Garmin Connect, to name just a few. Whichever method you choose to use, the important thing is to keep some sort of diary. You will be amazed at the motivation it provides, as well as its ability to highlight where your training is consistent, and where it's not.

IT'S JUST 'PLAN A' – ADAPTABILITY

Another important principle you need to be aware of when it comes to your training plan is that it is exactly that: a plan. It's 'Plan A'. You need to be flexible with it. Without a plan you don't have anything to work from, but while the plan is essential, you also have to be prepared to be adaptable when required. Just as you will have to be adaptable in your Ironman race. What are some of the things that will come up that require an adaptable plan? In a word: life ... work, travel, weather (especially hot and wet days), unexpected fatigue, illness, family and kids, and on it goes.

You also need to be adaptable within your training sets. Not every set is going to go to plan. Look at what is the goal or focus of the set. And from there execute the set as well as you can. Are you building your aerobic engine, your anaerobic ability, your swim, bike or run strength or maybe developing your knowledge around race nutrition? The outcome of the set could also be said to be its goal. If you focus on this goal, you'll be able to make the right adaptations when things don't go exactly to plan. Bad sets happen, so don't let it get you down. Bounce back and hit the next set. Momentum is on your side.

The training sets are designed to be completed all around the world. But if your unique environment and circumstances require modification, then all we ask is that you complete the set to the best of your ability and try to achieve its particular focus or outcome. If at first you don't feel you are doing it 'right', don't worry. Continue to put in your best effort and you will make progress, you will continue to develop, and you will be smashing your training sets and Ironman ambitions in no time.

While we're on the subject of flexibility, I think it's time to bring up the subject of injuries. Your training is like a house of cards. You want it to be big, really big, but you have to be careful. If you injure yourself, it's like taking a card out – the whole structure comes crashing down. Result? Weeks or even months off training. A much better approach is to be slow, thorough and make sure your house is strong. Rarely do injuries 'just happen'; there are usually warning signs, or you bring them on by deciding to break the rules. If warning signs appear, it's better to slow down and take the necessary action to prevent the problem. A few days off training now and appropriate prevention (that's why that team is in place) is much better than forging ahead. You want to arrive at the start line with a big, strong card tower, not one that's a heap of crumpled cardboard!

Illness must be treated in much the same way as injury, but is often unavoidable. Luckily, however, it generally lasts for a much shorter period. If illness strikes, you won't be able to continue with your original plan. Modifications will need to be made and new parameters put in place. You will need to take days off training to allow your body to repair and recoup. After this time training may be resumed, initially in a modified form, before a full training load can be resumed. Oh, and yes, you will be grumpy during this time – every triathlete is! But if you're this grumpy when you're ill, imagine how grumpy you will be if you dice with danger and bring the house of cards crashing down with no one to blame but yourself!

PERIODISATION – WORKING BACKWARDS FROM YOUR GOAL

Periodisation is a fancy name for the sequential, systematic and structured approach to your training program. In particular, it takes into account how the body adapts physiologically – that is, how your

Ironman body adapts to training – and creates a structure that works with and maximises this process. As part of this structure, periodisation includes times of loading and unloading the body, plus a taper (recovery and reduced training load prior to racing).

Understanding periodisation helps us to design an Ironman training program that allows an individual to reach an optimal level of fitness for their goal race. While it can become quite involved for elite athletes, the basics of periodisation are easy to grasp, highly relevant and very useful for athletes who class themselves as beginner or intermediate Ironman athletes chasing the Kona dream.

The five basics of periodisation are:

1. Weekly loading and recovery
2. Monthly loading and recovery
3. Structured approach to build up aerobic capacity
4. Structured approach to increase anaerobic threshold
5. Structured taper before the race.

To assist the triathlete in achieving their goals and to help periodisation be more effective, a segmented structure is used to build a training program. A complete program leading into a race or event is made up of blocks of training, and as you know, it's blocks of training that deliver results, not standalone training sets or one great week of training. Blocks of training are made up of weeks of training, which at the simplest level are made up of individual training sets. These individual training sets need to be scheduled in a way that allows them to be completed week on week. Applying all these concepts together forms the basis of periodisation.

The structure is sometimes given fancy names, such as microcycle, mesocycle and macrocycle, to give coaches a common language to use when discussing training plans. The time periods in each cycle (segment of training) can vary based on how you or a coach wants to structure the plan. Some elite athletes who don't have to work, and who train as their main 'job', might use an eight-day or ten-day cycle. However, most Ironman athletes conform to a seven-day week to accommodate the demands of kids, work and a 'normal' life. Therefore, all plans detailed in this book work with a seven-day week as the short-term plan. This is then expanded to a four-week (one month) block, which is the medium-term plan. The long-term plan is the 24-week plan that leads up to race day.

Planning is all about beginning with the end in mind. When you plan something, anything, you have to start with your goal in mind and work backwards. What do you need to achieve in training to give you the confidence that you will have a great race? This becomes your end point and what you're aiming for in training. You then need to work gradually and systematically back from this point, week by week. Now, there are some obvious problems with this approach if you go it alone. You don't have the experience of having qualified for Kona before, and possibly don't have years and years of endurance events or triathlon under your belt. This means a piece of the puzzle is missing. If it weren't I doubt you would be reading this book because you would already have qualified! Conveniently, that's where this book and working with a coach or mentor comes in – to help fill in those blanks and provide insight into the things that you don't know, because often enough you don't even know just how much you don't know!

YOUR JOURNEY

With the previous point in mind, it can be a powerful exercise to write down where you think your end points needs to be. The two key questions to ask are:

1. What do you need to achieve as your final peak sets for each discipline?

2. What else needs to be covered in your training plan to give you confidence that you will have a great race?

After completing your list, take a moment to reflect on what has been covered so far. No doubt you have included many points in your list that would not have been there prior to reading this book. Assuming this is the case (shoot, we hope so) that is fantastic and helps to demonstrate how much progress you have already made!

᎐᎐ ᎐᎐ ᎐᎐ ᎐᎐

Now you understand why it's so important to have a plan. Moreover, you know that your training plan is just that – a plan – and you're prepared to be flexible and adapt it where necessary. You understand the concept of periodisation and how you need to keep your eyes on the prize – finishing your best Ironman – and accept that your training will take a gradual, systematic approach that will build on itself week after week in the lead-up to your race. The next step is to dive into understanding the short, medium and long-term plans. You're almost there!

CHAPTER 11

BUILD AND ADAPT YOUR PLAN

At last, the moment you have been waiting for since Chapter 1 has arrived! This book is called *Journey to Kona* for a reason. It's the journey towards your best Ironman that will allow you to qualify for the elusive Ironman World Championships in Hawaii, and in this chapter we'll begin to map out the 24-week preparation that will see you through the race and crossing the finish line with all the glorious emotions that accompany such an achievement. We'll look at plans in the context of the short, medium and long term, learn what to expect from each phase, and understand how they fit together to create the six months of preparation you need leading up to your Ironman. Most importantly, we'll also learn the art of adapting plans. It's important to have this knowledge so that you can take the detailed plan provided in the appendices of this book and tailor it to your specific needs.

TRIATHLON PLANNING CONCEPTS – THE INTERPLAY

It is important before we continue that we again revisit the interplay between disciplines. While triathlon is made up of three unique sports, it is not a swimming race, a bike race and a run race. It is a triathlon race! Let me explain. You cannot prepare for each discipline like it is a standalone event. You need to look at the big picture and prepare for an Ironman triathlon event. Ironman is a unique event in itself. This means that when we are preparing your training program we have to take a different approach from the one we would use if you were training for a single-discipline event such as a marathon, bike race or open water swimming race. We have to sacrifice the performance you would be able to achieve in a single-discipline event in order to improve your performance as a whole – in other words, your performance as a *triathlete*.

Any intensity set in any discipline fatigues the body. As a result, an Ironman training program has to be set up to allow the body to recover from a solid training set before being fatigued again. It must also look at the way this fatigue accumulates as well as how it affects the next or subsequent training sets. Collectively it becomes a balancing act between building each discipline so you can have your best race, allowing sufficient recovery so the body does not break, and balancing the training sets to maximise this outcome. Let's get to it.

SHORT-TERM PLAN (WEEK)

The short-term plan fits within a seven-day period. In other words, it's your weekly plan. Within the weekly plan, you need to understand how the various sets play off against one another. This helps to manage the weekly load and also manage the interplay that exists between swim, bike and run that was discussed above. You don't want to have all your swims in a group, all your rides in a group and all your runs in a group. Additionally we need to disperse the fatigue placed on the body over the week.

Further, you need to understand what an anchor set is, and how this forms the starting point for developing your weekly plan. An anchor set is a training set that must occur on a particular day. This could be for one of a number of reasons. For instance, you may train with a triathlon group every Saturday or Sunday morning or maybe you have a run or swim partner you train with every Wednesday night at 6pm, and this set is always an interval set. These sets are not something that can be easily shifted, as you're unlikely to convince an entire triathlon squad to change nights just to accommodate you! As such, this particular set becomes an anchor set.

Many people find that their long ride is one of their anchor sets. The long ride often has to occur when you have more time available, such as on the weekend or a particular weekday when you don't work. As this is the most important set of the week and requires more time, it is also considered an anchor set.

Once you have determined one or two (and for some people three) anchor sets, you can plan the rest of the week's training around them. In doing that planning, a few training rules need to be observed:

1. Ideally you want to spread your disciplines across the week. For example, we don't want a long run followed by your hard run in the next session.

2. Ideally you want to intersperse your hard intense sessions with lighter sessions so that they are not occurring one after another or on the same day.

3. You need balance across the week, so that all your training does not occur over only a few days.

4. Recovery needs to be taken into consideration as part of the weekly and monthly cycle. This is discussed later in this chapter.

Here are some examples of how you could structure the plan, each with a different anchor set/s:

OPTION 1: FRIDAY LONG BIKE

Six sessions per week

Something like this is often seen when kids are thrown into the mix!

M	T	W	T	F	S	S
Intensity swim	Intensity bike	Swim long/ strength	Intensity run (PM)	Long bike	Recovery day	Long run

OPTION 2: MID-WEEK LONG BIKE ON A DAY OFF FROM WORK WITH THURSDAY INTENSITY SET COMPLETED WITH A RUN GROUP

Six Sessions per week

M	T	W	T	F	S	S
Intensity swim	No work – long bike	Recovery day	Intensity run with run group	Long/ strength swim	Intensity bike	Long run

OPTION 3: BELLS AND WHISTLES FOR THE WEEKEND WARRIOR – SATURDAY LONG BIKE

Ten sessions per week

M	T	W	T	F	S	S
Recovery/ technique swim	Intensity bike (AM) Just-for-fun run (PM)	Intensity swim (AM) Just-for-fun bike (PM)	Strength bike (AM) Intensity run (PM)	Long/ strength swim	Long bike	Long run

WHEN THE PROVERBIAL HITS THE FAN – HOW TO ADAPT YOUR PLAN

What we have discussed above is the ideal, but life will get in the way at some point and the best-laid plans will need to be modified or adapted. This could be for any one of a number of reasons: illness, unexpected work trips or issues with the kids, to name a few. As we discussed in the previous chapter, a plan is just that – a plan – and it needs to be adaptable.

If a set is missed the first option is to rearrange the plan. Sometimes a simple swap is all that's required, at other times you can add a 'make-up' session elsewhere in the week, but often a session will need to be dropped altogether to ensure you're not putting yourself at risk of injury and over-training. When this happens, an understanding of how to restructure your week according to the training hierarchy, outlined below, is essential.

Training hierarchy:

1. Long sessions (bike and run)
2. Intensity sessions (bike and run)
3. Strength session (bike)
4. Swim (drop either the long or the intensity session, not both!)
5. Just-for-fun (bike or run)
6. Recovery/ technique session

If sessions need to be dropped, they should be dropped from the hierarchy from the bottom up. In other words, the first set that should be dropped is the recovery set. If another needs to be dropped it should be the just-for-fun sessions, and so on. Of course, the day or days that you need to take off to fulfil unexpected commitments may not nicely match up with your triathlon plan. This means that the training week may need to be restructured slightly to allow the least important set to be dropped and the more important sets to remain.

Let's look at an example of a not-so-easy swap involving Option 3, which allows the triathlete to maintain their training program. Should the triathlete have work commitments that require them to have the Wednesday off training, their intensity swim and just-for-fun bike would have to shift. But they cannot simply be shifted to a Tuesday or Thursday because of other intensity sessions on these days, so we need to look to one of the other days of the week. Given fatigue levels are likely to be quite high after the weekend training sessions, it is a better bet to shift the long swim to the Monday and free up Friday for the intensity. This approach also means you are less likely to affect the intensity bike the following day. The training week would be rearranged to look as follows:

ORIGINAL TRAINING WEEK

Ten sessions per week

M	T	W	T	F	S	S
Recover/ technique swim	Intensity bike (AM) Just-for-fun run (PM)	Intensity swim (AM) Just-for-fun bike (PM)	Strength bike (AM) Intensity run (PM)	Long/ strength swim	Long bike	Long run

NEW RESTRUCTURED TRAINING WEEK

Ten sessions per week

M	T	W	T	F	S	S
Just-for-fun bike (AM) Long swim (PM)	Intensity bike (AM) Just-for-fun run (PM)	Day off	Intensity run (AM) Strength bike (PM)	Intensity swim	Long bike	Long run Recovery/technique swim (PM)

It may not be possible to rearrange the plan like this, and this is simply one example of a range of possible new plans. Let's look at another one.

Training on a Monday may simply be impossible – the triathlete may have to drop kids at school early in the morning and have an important work meeting that they know is going to run way past 5pm. And they know there's no way they're going to get their planned day off this week. Completing a solid day's training through the week on a different day is simply out of the question. This would require a different approach. With Monday training not an option, we could look to complete the following:

ORIGINAL TRAINING WEEK

Ten sessions per week

M	T	W	T	F	S	S
Recovery/technique Swim	Intensity bike (AM) Just-for-fun Run (PM)	Intensity swim (AM) Just-for-fun bike (PM)	Strength bike (AM) Intensity run (PM)	Long/strength swim	Long bike	Long run

NEW RESTRUCTURED TRAINING WEEK

Ten sessions per week

M	T	W	T	F	S	S
Day off	Intensity bike (AM) Just-for-fun run (PM)	Day off	Intensity run (AM) Strength bike (PM)	Intensity swim (AM)	Long bike	Long run

The benefit of this approach is that the triathlete manages to complete the best mix of training sets for the week. However, their long strength swim can't be maintained. This session has been dropped because, in the scheme of the overall triathlon, the swim takes the least time and the triathlete stands to lose the least from dropping this set. A mistake that many triathletes make is that they feel they should make up a set just because it is on their 'plan'. But you can only do your best, so don't worry if you can't create the perfect schedule every week. Maintaining appropriate weekly triathlon programming is the best option in this instance, as you don't want to adversely affect the following week of training, risk injury, or risk over-training because you have completed too many sets in too few days. Remember, it's about being as consistent as you can over the long term, not one perfect week.

MEDIUM-TERM PLAN – FOUR WEEKS (MONTH)

The next range of planning that you need to take into consideration is the medium-term or four-week plan. Conveniently, this is roughly equal to a month; however, for the sake of consistency month on month, it's best to work on a four-week block.

With the medium-term plan you need to be aware of loading and unloading the body. The full plan leading up to your race is developed off three weeks of building, followed by a recovery week. This allows a good balance for most triathletes, with sufficient load being developed before a greater period of recovery is planned. It's important to note that a recovery week does not mean *no* training. During this week, we simply unload the body *relative* to the workload it has been completing.

This reduced loading is beneficial for a number of reasons.

- It helps to prevent injuries by giving the body a chance to recover.

- It allows a period of mental recovery through planned days off from training – yes, you are allowed days off and they're great for you mentally!

- It allows the triathlete to plan their maintenance sessions. This could be a monthly massage or visit to a health care provider – remember that team! This approach allows triathletes to be organised, and being an Ironman athlete you have to be organised. You know when your recovery week will occur and can track forward. With this planning in place you are able to book your appointments in advance, knowing they will easily fit into your triathlon schedule, and harmony reigns in the life of the Ironman athlete.

- Long-term consistency is maintained – that golden rule!

- You hit the following week reinvigorated and roaring to get back into training again.

Once a regular triathlon program has been established, you will find that taking one or two days off will make a huge difference. It's important to remember that the purpose of the recovery week is to recover, but you should expect some fatigue from training to remain. This is very different from a taper period, which is discussed in the next chapter. A word of caution: while you may not notice this fatigue, it will be present. Often triathletes don't notice it because they have become accustomed to it!

The aim of the recovery period is to reduce the training load, but at a minimum you need to retain the key long sets. Depending on your weekly structure, this often means having a reduced load through the week. One or, if needed, two easy recovery days replace the intensity sets during the week, but the weekend long bike and run are retained. It's also important to have one day completely free of training in this time, as outlined below.

Now let's look at how this works by taking Option 3 from earlier in this chapter – Saturday long bike, and a total of ten sessions per week.

ORIGINAL TRAINING WEEK

Ten sessions per week

M	T	W	T	F	S	S
Recovery/ technique swim	Intensity bike (AM) Just-for-fun run (PM)	Intensity swim (AM) Just-for-fun bike (PM)	Strength bike (AM) Intensity run (PM)	Long/ strength swim	Long bike	Long run

IMPLEMENTATION OF A RECOVERY WEEK

Ten sessions per week

M	T	W	T	F	S	S
Day off	Day off or *optional technique swim or just-for-fun bike	Intensity bike (AM)	Strength bike (AM) Intensity run (PM)	Long/strength swim	Long bike	Long run

The above schedule allows the triathlete the flexibility to determine the length of recovery needed. Let's investigate this further. Monday is typically an easier day. Monday was originally an easy technique swim day, but it's now a day off to give some mental down-time as we progress towards our Ironman. This additionally allows a day to schedule any necessary appointments. Tuesday is now kept as an easier day as well, with an optional recovery set. Lastly, Wednesday's set has been changed. It is now an intensity bike with the afternoon bike being dropped. This decreases the overall load placed on the body for this day, while maintaining the key bike intensity set and the consistency of the program. Thus, over the first two days of the week, the fatigue the triathlete experiences decreases significantly.

To allow all of this to happen the key intensity swim has been dropped. While it would be great if this could remain, sacrifices need to be made. It's not that we have anything against swimming, but as mentioned earlier the time required to complete the swim is less than the time required to complete the other two legs, thus it carries less significance for most people. Of course, there are exceptions to this rule. If you come from a riding or running back ground but find the swim challenging, it may be better to rework the program so the swim remains.

This is, in essence, giving the triathlete two days without a large volume. By the end of this time most triathletes will feel like they've had a sufficient break and be re-energised and ready to go again.

There is also a contingency plan in place should they feel like they need additional recovery. If this is the case, the Friday swim can be modified to an easy technique swim or a morning off. This makes it possible for the triathlete to have up to three full days off over the week, if required. However, it's important that some training continues during this time, as you don't want to leave the body feeling lethargic. The benefit of this approach is that it has the triathlete ready to tackle their long weekend ride – the most important set of the week, and generally the Ironman athlete's favourite.

LONG-TERM PLAN

The long-term plan is the focused training that you begin when you're working towards your goal race. Prior to the start of the Ironman training program, it's best if you have been training regularly; it is not recommended that you start from scratch. If the gap between your current training volume and the first week of the 24-week program is too large, you risk injury: the chasm you are attempting to leap across is simply too wide. If you have not been training consistently, then you would need to complete a bridging program to put regular training in place before starting the 24-week program.

One of the common misconceptions within the Ironman triathlon community is the belief that it is only what you do in the last twelve weeks leading into your race that counts. While the last twelve weeks may be pivotal, what can be achieved in that time depends on what the triathlete has put in place in the previous twelve weeks. And to extrapolate that, what can be achieved in those twelve weeks is based upon your lifetime experience as a triathlete. Without a solid foundation in place, you cannot build the mansion that goes on top!

The long-term plan works with a 24-week block. The long-term plan is an important concept to understand, as it takes into account how the body responds to various training stimuli. As a result, this gives the plan distinct phases. These phases are sometimes given different names by different coaches, but the essence and objective of each phase is the same. These phases and their main objectives are:

BASE PHASE – build the aerobic base of the Ironman triathlete.

BUILD PHASE – incorporate more threshold and race-pace efforts to greater simulate and prepare the body for race day.

PEAKING PHASE – put the icing on the cake.

TAPER PHASE – allow the body to recover from the fatigue it has experienced prior to event day (discussed at length in Chapter 12).

RACE OR EVENT DAY – the fun bit!

Structuring training in this manner has additional benefits for the Ironman triathlete, in that it helps to break what is a considerable period of time into distinct and achievable chunks. This focuses your attention, and helps to decrease anxiety and the feeling that you're not going to be ready come race day. It also gives you the confidence that you're doing the right types of training at the right times.

When you then look at the 24-week program, you'll see that there are two distinct parts. During the first twelve weeks, you're ensuring that you will have the aerobic engine required to power you through the entirety of the coming race. In the final twelve weeks, with your 'engine' installed and working reliably, you can develop your ability to complete the distance at an improved pace. This is all relative to the individual and their personal pace, but the structure allows the program to be relevant for everyone from the slowest to the fastest triathlete.

Two key points to be aware of with the long-term plan are that the phases are based upon how the body responds to training, and this affects the types of training that you complete in each phase. Yes, the last twelve weeks are important, but you need a solid foundation upon which to build your mansion. Improving your endurance training ability is a slow process, but gains are available to anyone who is prepared to consistently and fully commit to the long-term plan.

Beyond the long-term plan you have the **Annual plan**, and this takes into account a **Recovery and transition phase**. This phase is needed for mental down-time and physical recovery from the race. Race recovery is investigated in Chapter 12 to provide some guidance on how to bring an annihilated body back to life.

RECOVERY

It is vital that the Ironman triathlete understands that it's during recovery and rest that the body makes the adaptations to the exercise that has been performed. During training and exercise, you are breaking the muscles down. The muscles recover from this and repair themselves when you're at rest – this is when an improvement in your physical condition actually happens. This means that sufficient recovery time needs to be in place. Without it, you are simply loading up the body without giving it a chance to come back stronger.

Recovery takes various forms within the training plan and is all relative to the individual. For an experienced triathlete, a recovery day may involve completing a recovery swim or ride, while for someone who is newer to training a recovery day may be a day entirely free of training. And note that recovery needs to be included in the short-term plan as well as the medium-term plan. To recap the earlier discussion, in the short-term plan, recovery days need to be planned and the higher volume days need to be separated. In the medium-term plan, developing an easier week of training every three weeks is very beneficial to the Ironman athlete.

Recovery sessions are included in the training program provided in the appendices of this book, and the recovery techniques you should use during these sessions are described below. If you have been prescribed exercise by a physiotherapist, these should also be undertaken during this time (and of course more frequently if they advise). Undertaking a short recovery session up to three times a week will go a long way to ensuring that you are fighting fit when you come to race.

Beyond the inclusion of days off or recovery days in the Ironman program, there are additional techniques that can be incorporated. The aim of these techniques is to aid in recovery and to help ensure that injuries do not occur by keeping the body, especially the muscles, supple and able to function.

The first and most important technique is one that triathletes find surprisingly hard to implement. Sleep! Ensuring that you get enough sleep is by far the best recovery method you have available; this is when the most repair occurs.

Additional to sleep, there are a range of manual manipulation techniques that can be used to enhance recovery. Two that need to be performed by a trained professional are remedial massage and dry needling. The need for a remedial massage therapist on your team has already been discussed; however, dry needling is also an excellent way to relieve tight, aching muscles. While remedial massage can be targeted, it's a shotgun approach when compared to the sniper-rifle approach of dry needling. This technique must be performed by a trained professional and is well worth consideration.

Beyond the professional services of remedial massage and dry needling, there are recovery techniques that the Ironman athlete can employ on their own. These include using a foam roller, massage ball, stretching and hitting the bath. As an Ironman triathlete you're constantly beating yourself up in the pool and on the road, in your intensity sets and on your long sets. You body needs some love! Ironman triathletes simply don't make time for these activities if they're not scheduled into the training program. The time taken does not need to be long and it should not be onerous, but it does need to happen.

Let's look at these DIY techniques in a bit more detail.

FOAM ROLLER – great for targeting the quads, calves and illiotibial band (ITB).

MASSAGE BALL – works best to dig into the glutes and hip flexors, and can be used on the bottom of your feet.

STRETCHING – this is an ongoing practice that must be undertaken regularly by the Ironman triathlete. It is recommended that triathletes target the following muscles:

- Calves
- Quads
- Glutes
- Hamstrings
- Hip flexors
- Triceps
- Pectorals
- Lats

THE BATH – this is a great way to help relieve the muscles. It provides a fantastic way to ensure the muscles are warm prior to a stretching session. Some people choose to use Epsom salts, and while there is little evidence that they help, why not? Throw some bubbles in, turn a podcast on and suddenly you have a great way to relax an athlete.

‹» ‹» ‹» ‹»

You have continued on your Kona journey and have built on your understanding of the key concepts of periodisation. You now understand how these affect the short, middle and long-term plan. You also understand that a plan is just that – a plan – and things won't always go to plan! To that end, you understand how to restructure the training week if needed. You also understand the importance of recovery and how this is structured within the program to ensure optimal outcomes for the Ironman athlete. But your understanding around recovery does not stop there; you have additional recovery techniques that may be used by the triathlete, which is what the next chapter is all about. We did say this was an Ironman journey!

CHAPTER 12

TAPERING

The taper is a period of prolonged recovery that allows the deep-set fatigue present in your body to disappear. A taper works because fatigue levels diminish at a faster rate than your fitness levels. This means that the fatigue you have become accustomed to training with disappears. While your fitness decreases slightly, it erodes at a much slower rate. This leaves you in fantastic shape to finish your best Ironman. Ironman triathletes who did not start their training plan early enough often overlook the need for this taper and decide to skip it. They feel that because their event is coming up, they must increase their training volume so they can feel confident about knowing they have done everything they can to have a great race. They often decide to complete their longest bike and run one weekend before their goal race. But this approach is fraught with danger. You can't cram for the Ironman test! The fatigue from completing your longest bike and run this late in a training plan will not completely disappear by the following weekend. As a result, triathletes who make this mistake start their event on tired legs, rather than being fresh and raring to go.

The added benefit of a taper period is that it allows you to mentally prepare for your event. With your training time decreased, there is more time to spend on ensuring that your nutrition plan, pacing plan and gear are all properly organised. It's often the case that you have to travel to the event, which takes additional time, energy and organisation. Having this extra time available helps to relieve the stress of rushing about at the last minute.

So, you might be wondering when the taper period begins. Over time it has become apparent that a reduced week of training, followed by a two-week taper, works best. This means that your biggest training week will occur four weeks out from your event.

Now let's look at each component of the taper in more detail. These components are the reduced week, the taper two weeks out from your race (Taper 2) and the final race week preparations (Taper 1). Your goal Ironman race will occur on the Sunday, and very occasionally on the Saturday.

That means it looks like this:

- Biggest week

- Reduced week

- Taper 2

- Taper 1 – race week with an Ironman event on the Saturday or Sunday.

REDUCED WEEK

The reduced week is far from an easy week. It simply involves a reduction in the training volume that you have been tackling. In this week you reduce the volume, but keep the key intensity sets in place. The other sets are modified or dropped to allow recovery after your biggest/peak week. By this stage there is little to gain by either increasing volume or maintaining a high volume. By contrast, you want to make sure that the training you're completing is all about quality with reference to your Ironman race. This reduced week forms a midway point between your biggest week and the start of your official taper period.

The other important point to note is that the end of this week is when travel will need to occur if your event involves a significant time zone shift, or climate or altitude change. Cough, cough... Hawaii! However, if the change is minimal, then travel can take place during either Taper 2 or Taper 1.

Following on from the example discussed in the previous chapter, the reduced week might look something like this:

M	T	W	T	F	S	S
Day off or recovery bike/ spin 20-30 minutes	Intensity bike	Intensity swim Stretch-ing	Strength bike (AM) Intensity run (PM) If needed the strength bike is dropped to allow additional recovery	Long/ strength swim	Reduced long bike Visu-alisation session	Reduced long run Stretch-ing

TAPER 2 – TWO WEEKS TILL RACE DAY

This is when the taper really starts and race mode kicks in. The last big set for Ironman athletes occurs in this period, ideally no closer than ten days out from the event. If you wish to complete a fitness test or time trial, this is the week when it should be done. While you will not be completely recovered when you undertake the fitness test, your fatigue will have diminished enough to allow an accurate test.

We're pretty certain your race will go well, but if you do make a goof ball of your race, the fitness test is a handy measure to reflect on. A fitness test is also useful if you want to compare your fitness across different races. Remember that Ironman races are highly variable in their nature, weather conditions, course (ascents and descents) and altitude. The fitness test gives you a standard measure so that you can compare your fitness leading into different races. We know you'll be back for more, so we're setting you up for long-term success should you wish to see your progress year on year.

While a fitness test can be great, as discussed in Chapter 4, you need to proceed with caution. The focus at this point in the training plan is on having a great race, and completing a fitness test comes a very distant second. There'll be a lot going on at this time that can stress you out, and if leaving out the fitness test will help you relax, then go ahead and leave it out. If you find you're attaching a lot of emotion and anxiety to the test – if you feel like you're walking into an exam – just skip it. For others, 'life' will turn on extra stressors – illness, family issues, work problems – and adding a fitness test to the mix will be an extra stress that you'd rather be without.

You may also find that you're unduly upset over a perceived poor result. If you do have a negative result, you need to frame it as just a small part of a bigger picture. However, if for *any* reason you think the fitness test could have a negative impact on the race, it should be dropped in favour of a standard intensity set or, if needed, additional recovery. In an ideal situation a fitness test will fit perfectly, but we are human beings, not robots. Keep your eye on the prize!

Ten to fourteen days out from race day there is little to gain from prolonged, hard training. While the longer training sets have already decreased in volume, at this point the intensity sets are also decreased. Your focus shifts to making sure your body is mentally and physically feeling great for the day. The training you do at this point is all about making sure your body is still ticking over. In this period you want to remind the energy systems, muscles – and your mind – that you have a job at hand. The plan is designed to provide just a little bit of stimulation, almost teasing the body. This prevents the body becoming lethargic and helps to settle the mind for the impending event. Some triathletes love taper time, but most hate it. They always feel they should be doing more and question their training. But because you have a structured Ironman training plan in place and have been following a process, you don't need to worry about this. All your hard work is done, and you are about to reap the benefits!

VISUALISATION

The time freed up by the reduction in training can be put to great use. This is the week that you ensure your mindset is in place. More than half the job has been done; you have tackled a training program that focuses on key Ironman training areas and tackled numerous challenges to develop your ability. Yet we have one more trick up our sleeve to help create the right mindset. This is the point at which visualisation sessions are built into the program. Let's look at visualisation in more detail.

Visualisation works because your mind does not realise that what you visualise is yet to occur; your mind thinks it has already happened.

This means that if you picture yourself overcoming challenges, you will know what to do when those same challenges get thrown at you in reality. Similarly, if you visualise having a perfect Ironman race, your mind will think that this has happened! And if you follow the program of planned visualisation, you're going to have your perfect Ironman race not once or twice, but eight times before you hit the start line!

There are three steps to the visualisation process:

1. See yourself having a perfect race.

2. See yourself encountering all the obstacles, challenges and concerns that you're worried about. However, as each obstacle presents itself, visualise yourself overcoming it and having a great race. In your imagination, work your way through a race that has every single imaginable problem, each of which fails to stop you. You recover and start swimming, cycling or running strongly again. You finish your dream Ironman and succeed!

3. Now complete your Ironman again. This time visualise yourself having a fantastic race where everything goes perfectly. This is what you finish your visualisation session with – your perfect race.

The visualisation session should take place at a time and place when you can be fully relaxed and won't be interrupted. Some people prefer to lie on their bed, others sit or lie on the couch, and some tackle their visualisation in the bath! The key is to be stress free, thus allowing your mind to vividly see your perfect race unfold. In total it's only going to take about 15-20 minutes for you to relax and work through each of the scenarios, but that's time well invested.

To intensify your visualisation, try to attach positive emotion to your race as it unfolds. For most people, what they see and feel, both physically and emotionally, provides the deepest experience. What do you smell? Enrich the experience; take a deep breath of the clean sea air. What do you see? Turn the colour up, make it rich and vibrant! What do you hear? Is it the sound of splashing or excited anticipation in the air? How does your body feel physically? You are strong, tenacious and capable. And most importantly, how does your body feel emotionally? Embrace the infectious energy that engulfs you! You can have your perfect race in your mind, and doing so will enable you to have your perfect race come D-day.

Again, following the example already discussed, Taper 2 would look something like this.

M	T	W	T	F	S	S
Day off or Recovery bike/spin 20-30 minutes	Bike fitness test	Swim fitness test or easy swim with some efforts Stretching	Run fitness test Visualisation session	Reduced long swim	Reduced long bike Visualisation session	Reduced long run Stretching

TAPER 1 – RACE WEEK

The last week before your big day follows a similar pattern to Taper 2. The volume and training stimulus drops further, with a few dabbles in intensity to keep the body awake and feeling fresh, and to ensure that lethargy doesn't set in. But while the training has dropped further, there are plenty of other tasks on the Ironman triathlete's mind.

Any necessary travel generally occurs at the start of this week, unless as discussed above there is a large time zone, altitude or climate change to manage. Naturally, the closer to home the race is, the later in the week the travel can safely take place. But keep in mind that check-in and race briefings often occur on the Thursday and Friday before the event, and you can't miss these.

Everyone's travel requirements will be different, and this affects each plan individually. Often training is dropped on the day or days of travel and substituted for a short walk or spin upon arrival to help loosen the legs.

Let's look at an example that assumes that travel occurs on the Tuesday. This means the week looks as follows:

M	T	W	T	F	S	S	M
Easy 20 minute run to keep the legs moving. Or day off to pack the bike and ensure all is ready to go	Travel followed by a short 20-minute walk or spin	Easy Zone 1/ Zone 2 run with short inten-sity seg-ments & stretch-ing Mas-sage if needed (recom-mended) but the massage must oc-cur after the run	Easy swim with short inten-sity seg-ments Visu-alisation session	Easy Zone 1/ Zone 2 spin with short inten-sity seg-ments Stretch-ing Carbo-hydrate-rich meal for dinner	Day off if you can cope or very easy 20-min-ute run Event check-in and race briefing CHO loading Optional visu-alisation session	Race day – the Ironman gradua-tion	Party time & recovery time

You're nearly there, but there is one final topic to discuss. This is the all-important topic of fuelling your body prior to race day. Of course, I'm talking about the concept of carbohydrate, or CHO, loading as discussed in Chapter 5.

CHO LOADING

While having a bulletproof nutrition plan for race day is important, you need to start thinking about nutrition a few days before that. You are going to expect something extra special of yourself on race day, which means you want to hit the start line with a full fuel tank. If you don't, you're going to have to ask more of your body while you race, which simply doesn't make sense. What does make sense is making it as easy on your body as possible. That's where CHO loading comes in. This is about ensuring your fuel sources are full to the brim, but you're not bloated. When you CHO load, you're ensuring that the glycogen stores in both your muscles and your liver are full – really full.

In a way similar to tracking and planning your CHO for your race, you need to calculate what you need to eat in the twenty-four hours before the race. Some people CHO load for a full forty-eight or seventy-two hours prior to the event, but I believe this is a little excessive as it can leave you feeling flat. The approach I'm going to outline is one that is completed during the twenty-four hours prior to race start, along with ensuring a CHO-rich meal the night before commencing the loading period.

Let's investigate this a little further. Two nights before the event, I recommend having a CHO-rich meal. This can be made up of pasta, rice, potato or your choice of another CHO-rich option. The main thing to ensure is that you have a normal meal for yourself, but one that has a significant component of CHO. Are you having a Caesar salad? No, it has to have a significant CHO source.

Part of the reason why just having a normal meal works is because you're tapering. This reduced workload means that your body is not requiring as much CHO as it did during the height of your training. The added benefit of this approach is that it allows you to relax up until the final morning prior to the race. When you wake the next morning, twenty-four hours prior to the race, the CHO loading starts and your approaching event gets real, very real! This action will change your mindset as you shift from training and taper mode to full race mode. Delaying this mindset shift as long as possible is a really positive thing to do – you won't benefit from increasing your stress levels earlier than this point.

So how much CHO should you be putting into your system during this period? Suzanne Girard Eberle, the author of *Endurance Sports Nutrition*, recommends that athletes carbohydrate-load in the range of 8–10g per kg per day for males, while females need to be slightly higher at 12g per kg per day.[24] For your final 24 hours, the day before race day, we need to use the following formula to calculate your recommended CHO intake.

MEN – WEIGHT IN KG X 10 = CHO CONSUMPTION

WOMEN – WEIGHT IN KG X 12 = CHO CONSUMPTION

24 Suzanne Girard Eberle, MS, RDN, CSSD, *Endurance Sports Nutrition – Fuel your body for optimal performance*, 3rd edn, Human Kinetics, 2014

If we apply this formula to a 65kg male, we get: 65 x 10 = 650g. This means that a 65kg male would be aiming to consume 650g of CHO over the entire day.

It may not sound like a lot, but if you don't do it correctly you will be eating an entire Christmas dinner party for one! The result? You rock up at the start line feeling like a baby elephant, which is clearly not ideal. So let's look at the tricks that experienced Ironman athletes use.

Follow a CHO-rich diet for the day, following your usual eating pattern. Let's assume this is breakfast, snack, lunch, snack, dinner. You then need a few additional items; the ones that give you a huge CHO bang for your buck. With your morning snack, have a sports drink; with lunch, power through 600ml of Coke or similar, and with your afternoon snack or dinner, have another 600ml sports drink. In short, you drink your carbohydrate. If, after you have calculated your CHO for the day and you think that you're going to be falling a little short, throw in a couple of lollies (candy) over the day, or have some supper before bed (fruit salad is a great option).

This format should have you easily meeting your CHO-loading needs. We also recommend that, the first few times you CHO load, you record what you eat to get a reference on your consumption. After undertaking the above procedure a few times, you will learn what's required to meet your needs, and this approach becomes a stress-free way to achieve your desired outcome.

A word of warning: notice that all the foods mentioned above were low in fibre and 'food bulk'. This is no accident. While you only CHO load for the final twenty-four hours, you want to be limiting your fibre intake for twenty-four to forty-eight hours before the race. Failure to do so can leave you shooting for the bathroom as the jostling effect of exercise, well, runs its course! Yes, I am aware that you normally eat the brown bread, the brown rice, the brown pasta, adore celery and have a triple kale smoothie with muesli for breakfast, but now is not the time!

In short, the essentials are: drink your carbohydrate, limit your fibre and aim to consume your body weight in kg x 10g or 12g-worth of CHO in the twenty-four hours prior to your race.

•꙳ ꙳• •꙳ ꙳•

Yee-haw! Suddenly you're one step closer! You now understand the taper period, including a reduced week, Taper 2 and Taper 1 – Race week. You understand that during this time training volume is decreased, but initially intensity remains. You understand where in the taper to implement a fitness test, but recognise that the objectives of this fall a distant second to the ultimate goal: a fantastic race day. Further to this, you understand that approximately ten days out is a key marker for the turning point in the program, as training excessively beyond this point does not increase your fitness on race day. Your mindset is going to be on-point because you're going to employ visualisation over the final two weeks of your Ironman plan. You are going to have your perfect race because you have seen it happen before!

CHAPTER 13

IRONMAN RACE DAY & BEYOND

All that's left to do now to get you started on your journey is to lock in your next race day, then turn to the end of the book, grab the plan and get out the door. But before you do that, I want to pass on all my tips on how to have a fantastic race day – the final hurdle. While you have all the knowledge, fitness and experience required to front up at the start line knowing that you will have your best race, it's certainly not going to be easy. It's going to challenge you. If this weren't the case, then everyone would be doing it and there would be little satisfaction in your goal. But you're about to put yourself among a select few who can say, 'I am an Ironman.' And among even fewer who can say, 'I've completed the Hawaii Ironman.' You will soon be able to wear that title with pride and have a bright shiny medal to prove it! You will have an experience you never forget, with stories to last a lifetime. You are coming to the conclusion of your journey and will reach the pinnacle as you run the last emotion-packed 100m of red carpet to the finish line. Imagine that feeling, a feeling of euphoria that no one can ever take away from you and only someone who has been there can relate to.

The final points that need to be covered to ensure your confidence come race day are: nutrition planning, preparing for transitions, negotiating aid stations and the inevitable race morning nerves. We'll also look at a post-race recovery plan and race evaluation so you can take as many lessons as possible from your Ironman and continue your improvement into Hawaii.

NUTRITION

It is recommended that you start undertaking your nutrition plan early in the race, while you still feel 'good'. By frontloading your nutrition, you can then ease back in the later stages of the race when you start to feel like you've been chewed up and spat out! This might mean that over the bike portion of the Ironman, you consume CHO at 10–15g per hour more than you do on the run. This works well because consuming nutrition when running can be more of a challenge. For example, you might start your consumption at 80g per hour, and drop this back to 65g per hour when you hit the run.

The nutrition choices we make early in the race are also different from what they are later. Ironman races generally start early in the morning, and consuming sports gels at 7:30am can be a bit much to handle. Our recommendation is to start with a formulated sports drink. While some can rely on liquid sports drinks for their entire race, others prefer to mix things up and include a sports bar or some solid foods. Later in the race when we hit the run, we can move to gels as these become easier to carry. If you anticipate being on course for a longer period, you may look to incorporate some savoury food within your nutrition plan. This helps prevent the issue of flavour fatigue, or getting sick of only having sweet foods or one type of food. This approach of using predominantly liquid foods and slightly decreasing your CHO intake on the run gives you the best chance of minimising possible nutrition problems.

Now let's revisit the nutrition planning introduced in Chapter 5, and build race preparation into the process.

1. Work out the number of hours that you anticipate you will bike and run for.

2. Work out the amount of CHO you would like to consume per hour (50–90g.) This may, for instance, be 80g on the bike and 65g on the run.

3. Lay out your nutrition for each hour of each leg in a separate pile. Be aware of what you intend to take from aid stations, and take this into account with your calculations.

4. Place your nutrition on your bike, in your bike bottles or in your run transition bag.

SPECIAL NEEDS BAG PREPARATION

Thought needs to be put into your special needs bag over the final few weeks of your training plan. Be mindful that some races require you to drop off your bags the day before the race, while some only require you to drop them off on race morning. This can affect the type of foods you can place in your special needs bag – perishable foods may not be suitable. Ideally you should sort out your special needs bags a few days before the event, then, if needed, finalise them just prior to dropping them off.

What goes into the bags will vary for everyone but, if you are planning on racing your best Ironman, it is recommended that you try to get though your race without needing to access these. If you choose to use them there are two broad categories that need to be catered for: nutrition and comfort. You can leave some items in appropriate bags for collection or use later. Items that fall into this category include, but are not limited to:

- Nutrition items
- Sunscreen
- Anti-chafe cream (Body Glide)
- Warm clothes if you're not sure whether you will need them. E.g. a wind vest or arm warmers in a cold race.

After your bags are all organised make sure to drop them at the appropriate location before the race. If you choose to use them, you don't want your emergency bags in the wrong location.

TRANSITIONS

Another critical part of your race prep is preparing for your transitions. An Ironman is long, but there is no point in burning time in transitions. Even so, it is not uncommon for triathletes to burn unnecessary time during these moments. If you do this you are sacrificing 'free time'. Two 10-minute transitions that should have been 3-4 minutes each makes a 12-14 minute difference to your overall time. That's the difference between qualifying and coming back the following year to have another crack!

First, let's look at the swim exit, which is the first point where triathletes often lose valuable time or waste needless energy. As you are approaching the finish of the swim, mentally think about what you are about to do – you have practised it before so this should be easy. With this thought in mind, keep swimming until your fingertips brush the ground – only when this happens should you stand up. If you stand up before this point the water will be too deep to run in and you will have to start swimming again or try to wade through deep water, both of which cost you valuable time and energy. Once you feel the brush of the bottom against your fingertips it's time to stand up and attack T1 as you have practised, which will be discussed next. The best mantra to say to yourself through each transition is 'smooth is fast.' We want you to be fast and have put everything in place to allow this, but you still need to be in control, or smooth, through transitions or else careless errors will occur. Now we'll look at rehearsing and managing T1 and T2.

When you rack your bike prior to the race, don't just shove it in your slot and turn your back on it. Instead, make sure you walk through the entire transition. This act of walking through transition as you will approach it on race day means that you mentally know where you are going and have been there and done it before. While it is illegal in triathlon to mark your bike or transition bag, for example with a colourful ribbon or some other easily identifiable marker, there are tricks that you can use to legally achieve the same result.

Start by the swim exit, then walk up the exit to the gear collection point and note where your bag is located. Keep in mind that not all the bags or bikes will be located there at this time, so things will look much more complex come race day. This is why we are walking through and rehearsing everything now.

From there walk though the change tent, then approach your bike in the same way that you will approach it on race day. Not being able to quickly find your bike is a common error among triathletes. Memorise which row number it is on and, importantly, which *side* of the row number it is on! From there walk down the row and find where your bike will be located. Now you need to look around for a marking feature. Running in transition and trying to find your bike is like trying to find a needle in a haystack, so try to find an easily identifiable pole, sign or other object (that wont be moved race morning) that you can run to. Then, from this point, you can easily locate your bike. This process saves time and gives you confidence. From your bike transition point, mock-walk the rest of your trip to the bike mount line and note where this point is. Bam, that's T1 done!

Now head over to the bike return. Trace the steps back to your bike rack or, if you know there are 'bike catchers' who will return your bike to your rack, follow your steps through to collect your T2 bag, through the change tent and then back out to the run exit. This mental rehearsal and walk-through is one of the 1% ers that saves you valuable minutes on race day.

NEGOTIATING AID STATIONS

Just as you want to be fast through transitions, you also want to move smoothly through aid stations. Smooth is fast. But this certainly does not mean that you are rushing. Just as importantly, we want you to remain focused on your end goal and be quick through the aid stations and if necessary bag drops, as this helps you to maintain a positive mindset. So let's look at how you go about achieving a smooth, speedy experience.

As you are coming into an aid station or bag drop, you need to think about and mentally prepare what you're going to do. This requires some on-course visualisation. Know the tasks you must complete and their likely order. This is especially important on the bike when aid stations fly by and you need to be aware of which area of the aid station you are going to be collecting your bottles from. Your tasks might look something like this:

ON THE BIKE

1. Collect water bottle.

2. Collect electrolyte bottle or bottle of Coke.

3. Refill/ replace bottles.

4. Throw discard bottles into the discard area.

5. Keep cycling.

ON THE RUN

1. Consume gel going into the aid station.

2. Drink one or two cups of water or refill water bottle.

3. Collect on-course nutrition. (Make sure you know exactly what you need, i.e. 1 x gel, 1 x sports bar, etc., but be equally prepared to be flexible if these are not available, which means knowing your approximate CHO values.)

4. Drink one or two cups of electrolyte or one cup of Coke.

5. Discard rubbish or used cups in the discard area.

6. Keep running.

THE START LINE AND HOW TO GET THERE ON TIME

Race day is now here. Don't expect to have a great sleep the night before. You will be nervous. If you have slept well, great, but if you haven't you're among the majority. Don't be concerned by this, as it's unlikely to affect your race day. It's the sleep that you get over the few days prior that matters.

When you wake up, food is again on the cards, despite having eaten plenty the day before. You need to top up that fuel tank. For breakfast the morning before the race, we need to consider foods that are in keeping with our CHO loading. They want to be low in fibre, high in CHO and easy to digest. Many will choose to steer clear of significant amounts of milk at this point, but this is really a personal preference. The alternative to milk is a couple of slices of white toast with honey, jam or vegemite. However, if you can tolerate milk, a low-fibre cereal will certainly do the trick. You may choose to have tea or coffee with this. This can be especially handy, as the caffeine can have the desirable effect of stimulating nervous bowels. A nervous, pre-race poop in the comfort of your own accommodation is much more desirable than waiting in a long portaloo line at race start. We did say that we were going to leave no stone unturned!

After eating I recommend going for a short walk or jog. Just for ten to fifteen minutes. This has a twofold effect: it helps your legs to wake up after sleeping and gives you time to focus on the task at hand. You are likely to know many people at the race and this will probably be the only solitude you enjoy for the day. At the start line there will be people everywhere, many wanting your time. People will be wishing you well and there will be training partners that you will talk to. You have a bike to check and set up, sun cream and a wetsuit to put on and a warm-up to complete.

There will also be plenty of 'noise' leading into the race. You will hear it all around you; people will question you. What do I mean by this? The noise you are going to hear is whether you're prepared. People will question you on your training. How long was your longest bike? How many kilometres did you run? What's your nutrition plan? What's your pacing plan?

There are two main reasons people ask these questions. While they may not realise it, they're trying to get you to doubt your training, question yourself and question your self-belief. If they create this self-doubt in you, it makes them feel better. Why? Because they're not ready. They doubt their own training, their own preparation, their own lead-up. If they create doubt in you and your training, it makes them feel better.

So what do you do? Don't listen; ignore it and quiet your mind. You have done the training and have followed a specific Ironman training plan, you have given yourself an Ironman education; you are ready. Trust in your training, trust in the process you have been through, trust in what you have done and, above all, believe in yourself.

The last point we need to cover here is the start itself. Take it in. Remember it. You have worked hard for this moment and it's one of the best feelings in the world. Look around, feel the energy, remember your journey and how far you have come. Pinch yourself. You want this moment, this experience, burned into your memory. Being at the start line is an experience you never want to forget. Especially if it's the start line of your first Ironman or first time in Hawaii. It is truly amazing. Then wait and listen for the familiar horn or cannon that will send you on your way. After this, all that's left to do is enjoy the journey.

POST-RACE RECOVERY PLAN

While all you're going to want to do the day after you race is lie on the couch or sit in the coffee shop and swap stories, it's really important that you keep active. However, under no circumstances is a run suggested!

Initially being active means walking … lots of walking … and this then progresses to swimming and biking and finally running. This should be short and slow at first, but build in duration. You will also find that your pace will naturally pick up as life is breathed back into your legs. Guidance on how long to walk for and a suitable progression to swimming and cycling is provided in the recovery plan below. At this point, it's also worth revising the recovery options available to the Ironman athlete.

In the first few days after your Ironman, you're likely to be too sore to undertake the manual manipulation techniques discussed earlier, but after about four days these techniques can be employed. During the second week after your event, you should continue regular short, easy training and stretching and using the foam roller and massage ball, and also book in for a second massage. If you get the urge to train hard again, try to ignore it until at least ten days after your event and then build into it slowly. Equally, don't be scared to extend this no-training period out to a full two weeks if you feel you need it.

14-DAY POST-RACE RECOVERY PLAN

Day 1	Day 2	Day 3	Day 4	Day 5	Day 6	Day 7
Walk 20 minutes Light stretch-ing	Walk 20 minutes	Walk 30 minutes Light stretch-ing	Easy swim or light spin 30 minutes Massage	Walk 40 minutes Foam roller & massage ball can now be used	Easy Spin to the coffee shop to swap stories	Day off

Day 8	Day 9	Day 10	Day 11	Day 12	Day 13	Day 14
Walk 40 minutes Complete post-race evalua-tion (dis-cussed below)	Day off	Easy swim or light spin 30-40 minutes Foam roller & massage ball	Very easy 20-min-ute run Massage	Day off or easy swim	Easy Spin	Very easy 40-min-ute run

RACE EVALUATION

A post-race evaluation is a great way to gain valuable insight and allow additional improvement as you head for your next race, which,
all going well, will be… Kona! It is, however, not recommended that
you complete this immediately after your Ironman. You're likely to
be highly emotional during this time. It's much better to allow everything about the experience to sink in and review your race and
training about a week later. Raw emotion will have passed, but the
race will be recent enough to allow clarity.

It's important that you review both your race and your training. Regardless of whether you're happy or disappointed about the outcome of the race, take time to reflect on the entire journey. Especially look back on how far you have come – it is with this perspective that athletes gain clarity. They begin to fully appreciate what they have achieved in their training, and how far their self-belief has come. More often than not this correlates to amazing personal development in their life outside of triathlon. This is something you should be proud of!

When undertaking an evaluation, there is no need to make it difficult or long-winded. The aim is to use the experience to its full potential to allow maximum personal growth.

The following questions provide a useful guide to direct your thinking

1. Race details: you may include weather, overall time, age-group place, overall place

2. Brief recap of the day

3. Strengths

4. Focus areas for improvement

5. Interesting/other points

Areas to consider for strengths and areas for improvement include your training leading up to the race, and the race day itself. It's recommended that you take the time to fill in the evaluation form below. The items in the evaluation form are in no way exhaustive, nor will everything apply to you; they're simply to provide some guidance.

The first part is an overall evaluation using the questions from the above list, which is followed by a more focused evaluation that allows you to consider some areas that may have been overlooked.

OVERALL EVALUATION – SWIM/ BIKE/ RUN	
RACE	
Guiding question	**Notes**
Race details • Weather • Overall time • Age-group place • Overall place	
Brief race day recap	
Strengths	
Focus areas for improvement	
Interesting or additional points	

FOCUSED EVALUATION – SWIM		
Guiding area	Race day	Training prior
Swim game plan • Longest swim prior (time & distance) • Biggest swim week prior (time & distance) • Consistency achieved in training • Pacing plan • Fitness test (including best result achieved) • Recovery • Taper • Race simulation • Gear selection		
Swim body • Aerobic development • Anaerobic development • Swim strength • Stretching • Recovery practices • Massage • Physiotherapist or similar • Injuries		
Swim techniques • Cadence & efficiency • Pacing (implementation)		

FOCUSED EVALUATION – SWIM		
Guiding area	**Race day**	**Training prior**
Swim mindset • Belief in self • Attitude • Flow • Visualisation • Peak sensation		

FOCUSED EVALUATION – BIKE		
Guiding area	**Race day**	**Training prior**
Bike game plan • Longest bike prior (time & distance) • Biggest bike week prior (time & distance) • Consistency achieved in training • Nutrition plan • Pacing plan • Fitness test (including best result achieved) • Recovery • Taper • Race simulation • Gear selection		

FOCUSED EVALUATION – BIKE

Guiding area	Race day	Training prior
Bike body • Aerobic development • Anaerobic development • Bike strength • Stretching • Recovery practices • Massage • Physiotherapist or similar • Injuries		
Bike techniques • Cadence & efficiency • Pacing (implementation) • Nutrition (implementation)		
Bike mindset • Belief in self • Attitude • Flow • Visualisation • Peak sensation		

FOCUSED EVALUATION – RUN		
Guiding area	**Race day**	**Training prior**
Run game plan		
• Longest run prior (time & distance)		
• Biggest run week prior (time & distance)		
• Consistency achieved in training		
• Nutrition plan		
• Pacing plan		
• Fitness test (including best result achieved)		
• Recovery		
• Taper		
• Race simulation		
• Gear selection		
Run body		
• Aerobic development		
• Anaerobic development		
• Run strength		
• Stretching		
• Recovery practices		
• Massage		
• Physiotherapist or similar		
• Injuries		
Run techniques		
• Cadence & efficiency		
• Pacing (implementation)		
• Nutrition (implementation)		

FOCUSED EVALUATION – RUN		
Guiding area	Race day	Training prior
Run mindset • Belief in self • Attitude • Flow • Visualisation • Peak sensation		

Ready, set, go! You now have all the underpinning knowledge required to be successful in your Kona journey. Race day will be a breeze! Sure, there will be nerves and sure, it's going to challenge you, but trust in your training and yourself. You have now covered the final components needed. CHO loading: check. Aid stations: check. Finish line: check. Start line, 'Yep, I'm going to remember that one!' But as this won't be your last Ironman, you're going to be keen to get back to training soon. Kona will be calling! You're going to be keen to continue your journey, continue the fun and improve further and get ready for the biggest race of your life!

'And will you succeed? Yes, you will indeed, 98¾% guaranteed! Kid you'll move mountains!'[25]

25   Dr Seuss, *Oh, the places you'll go!*, Random House, 1990

CONCLUSION

You have now completed your journey to Kona! Go you! As you reflect on the journey, you might realise that you have already improved as a triathlete.

At this point we'd like you to take the quiz again, and compare your new score to your old score to see just how far you've come. The improvement in your score has come about because you have implemented the lessons, taken action and commenced an Ironman training plan to build on your Ironman training experience. All that's left is for you to attend your own Ironman graduation ceremony – the Ironman race where you complete your best Ironman. And as a reward for this race, you'll get to attend the roll down ceremony where you will accept your ticket to the Big Island. You will know you are going to complete the Hawaii Ironman!

And after that? First of all, celebrate what you have achieved. Celebrate that you are going to Hawaii. For many the accomplishment of making it to Hawaii and the elation that comes from this can be better than race day itself. Hawaii becomes the cherry on top. Savour both. Because after you have recovered from your Ironman, the hard work continues once again as you prepare for arguably the toughest single day race on the planet!

If you didn't qualify don't be disheartened. It takes many Ironman triathletes many races to understand, implement and ultimately master the concepts covered in this book. In this case it's back to training and choosing another Ironman to work towards. Many triathletes say that

Ironman is a metaphor for life. They want to know what else they're capable of, what else they can achieve. Their self-improvement in Ironman goes hand in hand with their self-improvement in life. Ironman is a way of life. And we know you wouldn't have it any other way.

This book was not written simply to be read. This book was written to give you confidence and self-belief in your Ironman training. It was written to get you out there swimming, biking and running, to allow you to dream big and achieve your impossible!

I also have a request. If you have found this book useful, recommend it to one other training partner so that they are able to improve their triathlon and chase their dreams. For this we say thank you for spreading the word.

For those who are willing to share their journey, we can't wait hear about your experience and follow your progress. My community at The Kona Journey would love you to share all your trials, tribulations and triumphs. Take photos along the way, especially at your graduation ceremony, so that we can share your happiness. You can post your photos here:

Facebook: https://www.facebook.com/thekonajourney

Instagram: thekonajourney #thekonajourney
#finishyourbestironman

Journey to Kona started with a sad story, but finishes with a very different one …

Emma cruised along the road, checking her watch; 27km was the number she saw illuminated. The next aid station was about 2km ahead; she was fast approaching the magic 30km mark and exceeding all her expectations. It was late afternoon and she was running well. She had started with confidence and that confidence had never left her.

She reflected on the start of her training, and asked herself: 'Why am I doing this? To prove to myself I can, and to show my kids that if they set their mind to a challenge, they can achieve it.' The journey had challenged and changed her and she had grown from it. She had grown both personally and in her understanding of Ironman training and what she was capable of. A grin rolled over her face; she now had an Ironman triathlon education and was about to pass her graduation test, she was about to hear two longed-for magic phrases: 'Emma, you are an Ironman. Emma, you are going to Hawaii!'

As the road started to climb she sailed effortlessly up the hill. Her pacing was flawless. She ran the usual checklist over her body. Hydration: check, going well. Nutrition: check, her nutrition plan was on song. She was feeling great and running strongly. As the emotion of the event swept over her, her grin was replaced by a broad smile as a tear ran down her face. She almost couldn't believe what she was about to achieve. The finish line was now becoming a reality. As she ran along she could see it in her mind. The cheers, the red carpet, the finish arch, a bright shiny finisher's medal and the realisation she was going to Hawaii! But more importantly, the smiles on her husband's and kids' faces of a dream achieved. It was all within reach. This chapter of her Ironman triathlon was coming to a close and boy, had she enjoyed the journey. With a smile still on her face, on she ran ...

But this is your story, not Emma's. You still need to write the final page. If you have entered your next Ironman triathlon, well done.

And if you entered this race while you were reading this book, I'm super proud of you. If you are yet to enter your first or next Ironman, this is your number one priority. Put this book down and go and do it now! What are you waiting for? It's time to make your dream a reality! The time is now...

Enjoy the Ironman journey!

GUIDE TO THE TRAINING PROGRAMS

Ensuring everything is in place prior to your goal race is a mammoth task. I've covered a lot of elements in this book – but how are you going to practise and refine them all into your training? With a plan, of course! The following program is all about a plan of action. A detailed plan that is developed to cater for your Ironman triathlon goals. A plan that also takes into account your many obligations in life and at work to create the balance you need for a long-term commitment to your training. This allows you to be a successful Ironman triathlete.

After reading this book, you have all the underpinning knowledge and understand the principles required to complete your Ironman training plan. All triathletes will come with different anchor sets, different prior experience and different lead-up races planned. The plan presented here is designed to accommodate the most common training needs – those of the weekend warrior. If the plan doesn't quite match your unique needs, then you're encouraged to identify the patterns, structure and processes that are used in the Ironman plan and that have been discussed throughout this book. Using the plan and your new-found Ironman education as a guide, you will need to make adjustments to the plan and modify it to fit your individual needs. I know you can do it!

HOW TO READ THE TRAINING PROGRAMS

The training programs are set out in table format so that you can take in the information at a glance. However, this means that a lot of abbreviations and symbols are used. They might even look like gobbledygook the first time you try to follow them. After a while, however, reading them will be a breeze. To that end, we've provided the following instructions, plus a glossary of the terms the tables contain.

The following instructions on how to read the training sets refer to the first intensity run set on the first Thursday of the first 24-week program in Appendix 1. So just find that set, and read through the following 'translation'. Everything will soon be crystal clear.

EASY, MEDIUM, HARD
- The title of the set.

60 minutes
- The approximate time taken to complete the set.

WARM-UP
- The instructions under this heading form your warm-up.

10 minutes Z1 building to Z2
- The first part of the warm-up is ten minutes spent building from Zone 1 to Zone 2.

2 x 3 minutes building over the 3 minutes to from Z2 to Z4

- The second part of the warm-up comprises two three-minute sets. In each set you build over the three minutes from Zone 2 intensity at the start to Zone 4 intensity at the end.

4 minutes Z2

- This indicates four minutes at Zone 2 to finish the set and allow you to prepare for the main part of the set, which comes next.

MAIN SET

- The instructions under this heading form your main set.

2 (3 x 5 minutes)

- The main set is made up of two sets, indicated by the figure 2 at the front of the brackets. Each set comprises three repetitions, each five minutes in duration, which is indicated by the figure 3 x 5 inside the brackets.

1. 5 minutes easy

- Signifies that the first (1) of the three reps is five minutes easy.

2. 5 minutes medium

- Signifies that the second (2) of the three reps is five minutes medium.

3. 5 minutes hard

- Signifies that the third (3) of the three reps is five minutes hard.

Repeat for a total of two reps

- Reminds you that you need to complete the above for a total of two reps.

COOL DOWN

The instructions under this heading form your cool down.

10 minutes easy Z1

- Just like it says, you should do ten minutes at Zone 1.

Walk and stretch as needed.

- A friendly reminder to walk and stretch if you have time.

GLOSSARY OF TERMS

EFFORTS – the component of training when you're training or working harder (the bit that requires more effort).

HR – heart rate.

REPS – repetitions; the number of efforts you will complete.

RI – rest interval; the recovery period between the efforts. Sometimes, and often when swimming, the rest interval is a complete rest, but normally it's an easy spin or jogging recovery.

STRIDES & SWIM THROUGHS – relaxed, faster-paced running or swimming. Not so hard that you're labouring, but you're moving freely and enjoying the increased pace.

WARNING

If the training volume in the first week of this plan is greater than 10% of your current volume, then a bridging program is recommended. In particular take note if it is the run volume that is greater than 10% of your current running volume, as due to the higher impact of running it is more likely to lead to injuries. Therefore any adjustment should be made over a period of time to reduce the chance of injury. Additionally, if you are concerned about injury from running at higher paces, the following plan will need to be modified and those higher paced efforts changed to efforts at a lower intensity level.

24 WEEKS TO IRONMAN
SATURDAY LONG BIKE RIDE

This plan and associated instructional
videos are available for purchase through
The Kona Journey website.

thekonajourney.net

Personal 1v1 Online Coaching is also available
to guide you on your Ironman journey.

Week 1:

**24 Weeks
to race day**

**BASE
PHASE 1**

Monday	Tuesday	Wednesday
Day off	**Bike (AM) intensity set**	**Swim – intensity set**
It is recommended that you look through the first week of training and refer to the intensity guide to ensure you're ready to hit the ground running!	*This set is best completed on a hill or, if a hill is unavailable, a stationary bike trainer.* *Warm-up* 10 minutes Z1 4 x 1-minute hard efforts on a 1-minute Z2 recovery 2 minutes Z2 *Main set* 5 x 5 minutes Z4 on an easy downhill recovery (2.5-3minute spin) back to your start position and repeat 20 minutes Z2 *Cool down* 10 minutes easy Z1 spin **Run – just-for-fun (PM)** 30 minutes easy	*Warm-up* 400m easy freestyle and backstroke – 75m freestyle, 25m backstroke 400m freestyle – 25m hard, 25m easy 200m easy Z2 freestyle *Main set* 10 x 200m freestyle on a 10-second RI as: 4 x 200m easy Z2 3 x 200m tempo Z3 2 x 200m threshold Z4 1 x 200m threshold+ Z5a *Cool down* 500m easy freestyle and backstroke – 75m freestyle, 25m backstroke **Bike – just-for-fun (PM)** 50 minutes easy

Thursday	Friday	Saturday	Sunday
Bike (AM) – strength set	**Swim – long/ strength**	**Long ride**	**Long run**
This set is best completed on a hill or, if a hill is unavailable, a stationary bike trainer		3 hours	90 minutes
	Warm-up 400m easy freestyle and backstroke – 75m freestyle, 25m backstroke	*Warm-up* 10 minutes Z1	*Warm-up* 10 minutes Z1
Warm-up 10 minutes Z1		*Main set* 2 hrs 45 mins: target Z1/2	10 minutes building to Z2
4 x 1-minute hard efforts on a 1-minute Z2 recovery	300m easy Z1 freestyle		*Main set* 65 minutes Z2
2 minutes Z2		*Cool down* 5 minutes easy Z1 spinning	
	200m freestyle – 75m Z2, 25m easy Z1		Include walk breaks when necessary. A couple of minutes every 20-60 minutes is recommended.
Main set 5 x 5 minutes Z2 low cadence (70-80 RPM) on an easy downhill recovery (2.5-3 minute spin) back to your start position and repeat	100m steady Z2 freestyle		
20 minutes Z2	*Main set* 9 x 150m Z2 on a 10-second RI as:		*Cool down* 5 minutes easy Z1 running
Cool down 10 minutes easy Z1 spin	1. Freestyle swim		
Run – easy, medium, hard (PM)	2. Freestyle with pull buoy		
60 minutes	3. Freestyle with pull buoy and paddles		
Warm-up 10 minutes Z1 building to Z2			
2 x 3 minutes building over the 3 minutes from Z2 to Z4	Repeat for a total of 3 sets.		
4 minutes Z2	*Cool down* 300m easy freestyle and backstroke –75m freestyle, 25m backstroke		
Main set *2 (3 x 5 minutes)* 1. minutes easy 2. minutes medium 3. minutes hard			
Repeat for a total of 2 sets			
Cool down 10 minutes easy Z1 running			
Walk and stretch as needed.			

Week 2:

23 Weeks
to race day

**BASE
PHASE 1**

Monday	Tuesday	Wednesday
Technique swim	**Bike fitness test (AM)**	**Swim – intensity set**

Monday

Technique swim

Warm-up
300m easy Z1 freestyle

200m freestyle – 75m Z2,
25m easy Z1

100m steady Z2 freestyle

Main set
10 x 50m as: 25m drill-of-choice 1 into 25m freestyle

Our go-to drills are:

- 6-1-6
- Javelin Drill
- Scull #1
- Scull #2
- Scull combo drill
- Waterpolo drill
- Doggy paddle drill
- Unco drill

A full list of suitable drills can be found at:
http://www.swimsmooth.com/drills

300m Z1 freestyle

10 x 50m as:
25m drill-of-choice 2 into 25 freestyle

300m Z1 freestyle

Cool down
200m Z1 freestyle

Tuesday

Bike fitness test (AM)

Refer to
Chapter 4

Run – just-for-fun (PM)

30 minutes easy

Wednesday

Swim – intensity set

Warm-up
400m easy freestyle and backstroke – 75m freestyle, 25m backstroke

400m freestyle – 25m hard, 25m easy

200m easy Z2 freestyle

Main set
10 x 200m freestyle on a 10-second RI as:

4 x 200m easy Z2
3 x 200m tempo Z3
2 x 200m threshold Z4
1 x 200m threshold+ Z5a

Cool down
500m easy freestyle and backstroke – 75m freestyle, 25m backstroke

Bike – Just-for-fun (PM)

50 minutes easy

Thursday	Friday	Saturday	Sunday
Bike (AM) – strength set	**Swim – long/ strength**	**Long ride**	**Long run**
This set is best completed on a hill or, if a hill is unavailable, a stationary bike trainer.	*Warm-up* 400m easy freestyle and backstroke – 75m freestyle, 25m backstroke	3hrs 30mins	90 minutes
		Warm-up 10 minutes Z1	*Warm-up* 10 minutes Z1
Warm-up 10 minutes Z1	300m easy Z1 freestyle	*Main set* 3 hrs 15 mins: target Z1/2	10 minutes building to Z2
4 x 1-minute hard efforts on a 1-minute Z2 recovery	200m freestyle – 75m Z2, 25m easy Z1	*Cool down* 5 minutes easy Z1 spinning	*Main set* 65 minutes Z2
2 minutes Z2	100m steady Z2 freestyle		Include walk breaks when necessary. A couple of minutes every 20-60 minutes is recommended.
Main set 5 x 4 minutes Z2 low cadence (70-80 RPM) on an easy downhill recovery (2.5-3 minute spin) back to your start position and repeat	*Main set* 9 x 150m Z2 on a 10-second RI as: 1. Freestyle swim 2. Freestyle with pull buoy 3. Freestyle with pull buoy and paddles		*Cool down* 5 minutes easy Z1 running
20 minutes Z2	Repeat for a total of 3 sets.		
Cool down 10 minutes easy Z1 spin	*Cool down* 500m easy freestyle and backstroke – 75m freestyle, 25m backstroke		
Run – fitness test			
Refer to Chapter 4			

Week 3:

22 Weeks to race day

BASE PHASE 1

	Monday	Tuesday	Wednesday
	Technique swim	**Bike (AM) strength set**	**Swim fitness test**
	Warm-up 300m easy Z1 freestyle	*This set is best completed on a hill or, if a hill is unavailable, a stationary bike trainer.*	Refer to Chapter 4
	200m freestyle – 75m Z2, 25m easy Z1	*Warm-up* 10 minutes Z1	**Bike – just-for-fun (PM)** 60 minutes easy
	100m steady Z2 freestyle	4 x 1-minute hard efforts on a 1-minute Z2 recovery	
	Main set 10 x 50m as: 25m drill-of-choice 1 into 25m freestyle	2 minutes Z2	
	300m Z1 freestyle	*Main set* 5 x 5 minutes Z2 low cadence (70-80 RPM) on an easy downhill recovery back to your start position and repeat	
	10 x 50m as: 25m drill-of-choice 2 into 25 freestyle		
	300m Z1 freestyle	20 minutes Z2	
	Cool down 200m Z1 freestyle	*Cool down* 10 minutes easy Z1 spin	
		Run – just-for-fun (PM) 30 minutes easy	

Thursday	Friday	Saturday	Sunday
Bike (AM) – strength set	**Swim – long/ strength**	**Long run**	**Long ride**
This set is best completed on a hill or, if a hill is unavailable, a stationary bike trainer.		100 minutes	3 hrs 30 mins
	Warm-up 400m easy freestyle and backstroke – 75m freestyle, 25m backstroke	*Warm-up* 10 minutes Z1	*Warm-up* 10 minutes Z1
Warm-up 10 minutes Z1		10 minutes building to Z2	*Main set* 3 hrs 15 mins: target Z1/2
4 x 1-minute hard efforts on a 1-minute Z2 recovery	300m easy Z1 freestyle	*Main set* 75 minutes Z2	*Cool down* 5 minutes easy Z1 spinning
2 minutes Z2	200m freestyle – 75m Z2, 25m easy Z1	Include walk breaks when necessary. A couple of minutes every 20-60 minutes is recommended.	
Main set 5 x 5 minutes Z2 low cadence (70-80 RPM) on an easy downhill recovery (2.5-3 minute spin) back to your start position and repeat	100m steady Z2 freestyle		
20 minutes Z2	*Main set* 9 x 200m Z2 on a 10-second RI as:	*Cool down* 5 minutes easy Z1 running	
Cool down 10 minutes easy Z1 spin	1. Freestyle swim		
Run – easy, medium, hard	2. Freestyle with pull buoy		
60 minutes	3. Freestyle with pull buoy and paddles		
Warm-up 10 minutes Z1 building to Z2			
2 x 3 minutes building over the 3 minutes from Z2 to Z4	Repeat for a total of 3 sets.		
4 minutes Z2	*Cool down* 500m easy freestyle and backstroke – 75m freestyle, 25m backstroke		
Main set **2 (3 x 5 minutes)** 1. 5 minutes easy 2. 5 minutes medium 3. 5 minutes hard			
Repeat for a total of 2 reps			
Cool down 10 minutes easy Z1 running			
Walk and stretch as needed.			

Week 4:

21 Weeks
to race day

**BASE
PHASE 1**

Recovery
Week

Monday	Tuesday	Wednesday
Day off	**Recovery swim or just-for-fun bike**	**Bike (AM) – strength set**

Tuesday

**Recovery swim
or just-for-fun bike**

Swim
Easy 40-50 minute   Z1
freestyle

Or

Bike
Easy 50-60 minute   Z1 spin

Wednesday

Bike (AM) – strength set
*This set is best completed
on a hill or, if a hill is
unavailable, a stationary
bike trainer.*

Warm-up
10 minutes Z1

4 x 1-minute hard
efforts on a 1-minute Z2
recovery

2 minutes Z2

Main set
5 x 5 minutes Z2 low
cadence (70-80 RPM) on
an easy downhill recovery
back to your start position
and repeat

20 minutes Z2

Cool down
10 minutes easy Z1 spin

Thursday	Friday	Saturday	Sunday
Bike (AM) – strength set	**Swim – long/ strength**	**Long ride**	**Long run**
This set is best completed on a hill or, if a hill is unavailable, a stationary bike trainer.		3 hrs 45 mins	110 minutes
	Warm-up	*Warm-up*	*Warm-up*
Warm-up	400m easy freestyle and backstroke –	10 minutes Z1	10 minutes Z1
10 minutes Z1	75m freestyle, 25m backstroke	*Main set*	10 minutes building to Z2
4 x 1-minute hard efforts on a 1-minute Z2 recovery	300m easy Z1 freestyle	3 hrs 30 mins: target Z1/2	*Main set*
		Cool down	85 minutes Z2
2 minutes Z2	200m freestyle – 75m Z2, 25m easy Z1	5 minutes easy Z1 spinning	Include walk breaks when necessary.
Main set			A couple of
5 x 5 minutes Z2 low cadence (70-80 RPM) on an easy downhill recovery (2.5-3 minute spin) back to your start position and repeat	100m steady Z2 freestyle		minutes every 20-60 minutes is recommended.
	Main set		*Cool down*
	9 x 200m Z2 on a 10-second RI as:		5 minutes easy Z1 running
	1. Freestyle swim		
20 minutes Z2	2. Freestyle with pull buoy		
Cool down	3. Freestyle with pull buoy and paddles		
10 minutes easy Z1 spin			
Run – tempo	Repeat for a total of 3 sets.		
Warm-up	*Cool down*		
10 minutes Z1	500m easy freestyle and backstroke – 75m freestyle, 25m backstroke		
10 minutes Z2			
Main set			
2 x 8 minutes Z3 on an easy 5-minute Z2 recovery			
Cool down			
5 minutes Z1			

Week 5:

20 Weeks
to race day

**BASE
PHASE 2**

Monday	Tuesday	Wednesday
Technique swim	**Bike (AM) strength set**	**Swim – intensity set**
Warm-up 300m easy Z1 freestyle	*This set is best completed on a hill or, if a hill is unavailable, a stationary bike trainer.*	*Warm-up* 400m easy freestyle and backstroke – 75m freestyle, 25m backstroke
200m freestyle – 75m Z2, 25m easy Z1	*Warm-up* 10 minutes Z1	
100m steady Z2 freestyle	4 x 1-minute hard efforts on a 1-minute Z2 recovery	400m freestyle – 25m hard, 25m easy
Main set 10 x 50m as: 25m drill-of-choice 1 into 25m freestyle	2 minutes Z2	200m easy Z2 freestyle
300m Z1 freestyle	*Main set* 5 x 6 minutes Z2 low cadence (70-80 RPM) on an easy downhill recovery back to your start position and repeat	*Main set* 10 x 200m freestyle on a 10-second RI as: 4 x 200m easy Z2 3 x 200m tempo Z3 2 x 200m threshold Z4 1 x 200m threshold+ Z5a
10 x 50m as: 25m drill-of-choice 2 into 25 freestyle		
300m Z1 freestyle	20 minutes Z2	*Cool down* 500m easy freestyle and backstroke – 75m freestyle, 25m backstroke
Cool down 200m Z1 freestyle	*Cool down* 10 minutes easy Z1 spin	
	Run – just-for-fun (PM)	**Bike – just-for-fun (PM)**
	40 minutes easy	60 minutes easy

Thursday	Friday	Saturday	Sunday
Bike (AM) – strength set	**Swim – long/ strength**	**Long ride**	**Long run**
This set is best completed on a hill or, if a hill is unavailable, a stationary bike trainer.		3 hrs 45mins	120 minutes
	Warm-up		
Warm-up	400m easy freestyle and backstroke –	*Warm-up*	*Warm-up*
10 minutes Z1	75m freestyle,	10 minutes Z1	10 minutes Z1
4 x 1-minute hard efforts on a 1-minute Z2 recovery	25m backstroke	*Main set* 3 hrs 30 mins: target Z1/2	10 minutes building to Z2
2 minutes Z2	300m easy Z1 freestyle	*Cool down* 5 minutes easy	*Main set* 95 minutes Z2
Main set 5 x 6 minutes Z2 low cadence (70-80 RPM) on an easy downhill recovery (2.5-3 minute spin) back to your start position and repeat	200m freestyle – 75m Z2, 25m easy Z1	Z1 spinning	Include walk breaks when necessary. A couple of minutes every 20-60 minutes is recommended.
20 minutes Z2	100m steady Z2 freestyle		
Cool down 10 minutes easy Z1 spin	*Main set* 9 x 200m Z2 on a 10-second RI as:		*Cool down* 5 minutes easy Z1 running
Run – 4 /3/2/1 fartlek set (PM)	1. Freestyle swim		
60 minutes	2. Freestyle with pull buoy		
Warm-up 10 minutes Z1 building to Z2	3. Freestyle with pull buoy and paddles		
4 x 1-minute strides on a 1-minute easy jogging recovery			
2 minutes Z2	Repeat for a total of 3 sets.		
Main set This set is all about learning your zones and how to vary your pace to match each. As you shift to a higher zone you should be running just a little harder.	*Cool down* 500m easy freestyle and backstroke – 75m freestyle, 25m backstroke		
4 minutes Z2 3 minutes Z3 2 minutes Z4 1 minute Z5b			
Repeat for a total of 4 sets.			
Cool down 10 minutes easy Z1 running			
Walk and stretch as needed.			

Week 6:

19 Weeks
to race day

**BASE
PHASE 2**

Monday	Tuesday	Wednesday
Technique swim	**Bike (AM) strength set**	**Swim – intensity set**

Technique swim

Warm-up
300m easy Z1 freestyle

200m freestyle – 75m
Z2, 25m easy Z1

100m steady Z2
freestyle

Main set
10 x 50m as:
25m drill-of-choice 1 into
25m freestyle

300m Z1 freestyle

10 x 50m as:
25m drill-of-choice 2 into
25 freestyle

300m Z1 freestyle

Cool down
200m Z1 freestyle

Bike (AM) strength set

*This set is best
completed on a hill or,
if a hill is unavailable, a
stationary bike trainer.*

Warm-up
10 minutes Z1

4 x 1-minute hard
efforts on a 1-minute Z2
recovery

2 minutes Z2

Main set
5 x 6 minutes Z2 low
cadence (70-80 RPM)
on an easy downhill
recovery back to your
start position and repeat

20 minutes Z2

Cool down
10 minutes easy Z1 spin

Run – just-for-fun (PM)

40 minutes easy

Swim – intensity set

Warm-up
400m easy freestyle
and backstroke –
75m freestyle,
25m backstroke

200m freestyle – 25m
hard, 25m easy

200m easy Z2 freestyle

Main set
10 x 250m freestyle on a
10-second RI as:
4 x 250m easy Z2
3 x 250m tempo Z3
2 x 250m threshold Z4
1 x 250m threshold+ Z5a

Cool down
500m easy freestyle
and backstroke –
75m freestyle,
25m backstroke

Bike – just-for-fun (PM)

60 minutes easy

Thursday	Friday	Saturday	Sunday
Bike (AM) – strength set	**Swim – long/ strength**	**Long ride**	**Long run**
This set is best completed on a hill or, if a hill is unavailable, a stationary bike trainer.	*Warm-up* 400m easy freestyle and backstroke – 75m freestyle, 25m backstroke	4 hours	120 minutes
		Warm-up 10 minutes Z1	*Warm-up* 10 minutes Z1
Warm-up 10 minutes Z1	300m easy Z1 freestyle	*Main set* 3 hrs 45 mins: target Z1/2	10 minutes building to Z2
4 x 1-minute hard efforts on a 1-minute Z2 recovery	200m freestyle – 75m Z2, 25m easy Z1	*Cool down* 5 minutes easy Z1 spinning	*Main set* 95 minutes Z2
2 minutes Z2	100m steady Z2 freestyle		Include walk breaks when necessary. A couple of minutes every 20-60 minutes is recommended.
Main set 5 x 5 minutes Z2 low cadence (70-80 RPM) on an easy downhill recovery (2.5-3 minute spin) back to your start position and repeat	*Main set* 9 x 200m Z2 on a 10-second RI as: 1. Freestyle swim 2. Freestyle with pull buoy		*Cool down* 5 minutes easy Z1 running
20 minutes Z2	3. Freestyle with pull buoy and paddles		
Cool down 10 minutes easy Z1 spin	Repeat for a total of 3 sets.		
Run – Build Set	*Cool down* 500m easy freestyle and backstroke – 75m freestyle, 25m backstroke		
Warm-up 10 minutes Z1			
10 minutes Z2			
Main set 20 minutes Z2 15 minutes Z3 10 minutes Z4			
Cool down 5 minutes Z1			

Week 7:

18 Weeks
to race day

**BASE
PHASE 2**

Monday	Tuesday	Wednesday
Technique swim	**Bike (AM) strength set**	**Swim – intensity set**
Warm-up 300m easy Z1 freestyle	*This set is best completed on a hill or, if a hill is unavailable, a stationary bike trainer.*	*Warm-up* 400m easy freestyle and backstroke – 75m freestyle, 25m backstroke
200m freestyle – 75m Z2, 25m easy Z1	*Warm-up* 10 minutes Z1	200m freestyle – 25m hard, 25m easy
100m steady Z2 freestyle	4 x 1-minute hard efforts on a 1-minute Z2 recovery	200m easy Z2 freestyle
Main set 10 x 50m as: 25m drill-of-choice 1 into 25m freestyle	2 minutes Z2	*Main set* 10 x 250m freestyle on a 10-second RI as:
300m Z1 freestyle	*Main set* 5 x 6 minutes Z2 low cadence (70-80 RPM) on an easy downhill recovery back to your start position and repeat	4 x 250m easy Z2 3 x 250m tempo Z3 2 x 250m threshold Z4 1 x 250m threshold+ Z5a
10 x 50m as: 25m drill-of-choice 2 into 25 freestyle	20 minutes Z2	*Cool down* 500m easy freestyle and backstroke – 75m freestyle, 25m backstroke
300m Z1 freestyle	*Cool down* 10 minutes easy Z1 spin	
Cool down 200m Z1 freestyle	**Run – just-for-fun (PM)**	**Bike – just-for-fun (PM)**
	40 minutes easy	70 minutes easy

Thursday	Friday	Saturday	Sunday
Bike (AM) – strength set	**Swim – long/ strength**	**Long run**	**Long ride**
This set is best completed on a hill or, if a hill is unavailable, a stationary bike trainer.		120 minutes	4 hours
	Warm-up		
Warm-up	400m easy freestyle and backstroke – 75m freestyle, 25m backstroke	*Warm-up* 10 minutes Z1	*Warm-up* 10 minutes Z1
10 minutes Z1		10 minutes building to Z2	*Main set* 3 hrs 45 mins: target Z1/2
4 x 1-minute hard efforts on a 1-minute Z2 recovery	300m easy Z1 freestyle	*Main set* 95 minutes Z2	Try to include a 30-minute Z3 effort.
2 minutes Z2	200m freestyle – 75m Z2 25m easy Z1	Include walk breaks when necessary. A couple of minutes every 20-60 minutes is recommended.	*Cool down* 5 minutes easy Z1 spinning
Main set 5 x 5 minutes Z2 low cadence (70-80 RPM) on an easy downhill recovery (2.5-3 minute spin) back to your start position and repeat	100m steady Z2 freestyle		
	Main set 9 x 200m Z2 on a 10-second RI as:		
20 minutes Z2	1. Freestyle swim	*Cool down* 5 minutes easy Z1 running	
Cool down 10 minutes easy Z1 spin	2. Freestyle with pull buoy		
Run – interval set *Warm-up* 10 minutes Z1	3. Freestyle with pull buoy and paddles		
4 x 1-minute hard (Z4)	Repeat for a total of 3 sets.		
1minute easy (Z2)	*Cool down* 500m easy freestyle and backstroke – 75m freestyle, 25m backstroke		
2 minutes Z2			
Main set 5 x 5 minutes Z4 on a 30-second easy Z1 recovery jog			
Cool down 10 minutes Z1			

Week 8:

17 Weeks
to race day

**BASE
PHASE 2**

Monday	Tuesday	Wednesday
Day off	**Recovery swim or just-for-fun bike** *Swim* Easy 40-50 minute Z1 freestyle Or *Bike* Easy 50-60 minute Z1 spin	**Bike (AM) – strength set** *This set is best completed on a hill or, if a hill is unavailable, a stationary bike trainer.* *Warm-up* 10 minutes Z1 4 x 1-minute hard efforts on a 1-minute Z2 recovery 2 minutes Z2 *Main set* 5 x 6 minutes Z2 low cadence (70-80 RPM) on an easy downhill recovery back to your start position and repeat 20 minutes Z2 *Cool down* 10 minutes easy Z1 spin

Thursday	Friday	Saturday	Sunday
Bike (AM) – strength set	**Swim – long/ strength**	**Long ride**	**Long run**
This set is best completed on a hill or, if a hill is unavailable, a stationary bike trainer.	*Warm-up* 400m easy freestyle and backstroke – 75m freestyle, 25m backstroke	4 hours	130 minutes
Warm-up 10 minutes Z1		*Warm-up* 10 minutes Z1	*Warm-up* 10 minutes Z1
4 x 1-minute hard efforts on a 1-minute Z2 recovery	300m easy Z1 freestyle	*Main set* 3hrs 45 mins: target Z1/2	10 minutes building to Z2
2 minutes Z2	200m freestyle – 75m Z2, 25m easy Z1	Try to include a 30-minute Z3 effort.	*Main set* 105 minutes Z2
Main set 5 x 5 minutes Z2 low cadence (70-80 RPM) on an easy downhill recovery (2.5-3-minute spin) back to your start position and repeat	100m steady Z2 freestyle	*Cool down* 5 minutes easy Z1 spinning	Include walk breaks when necessary. A couple of minutes every 20-60 minutes is recommended.
20 minutes Z2	*Main set* 9 x 200m Z2 on a 10-second RI as: 1. Freestyle swim 2. Freestyle with pull buoy 3. Freestyle with pull buoy and paddles		*Cool down* 5 minutes easy Z1 running
Cool down 10 minutes easy Z1 spin	Repeat for a total of 3 sets.		
Run – tempo	*Cool down* 500m easy freestyle and backstroke – 75m freestyle, 25m backstroke		
Warm-up 10 minutes Z1			
10 minutes Z2			
Main set 2 x 8 minutes Z3 on an easy 5-minute Z2 recovery			
Cool down 5 minutes Z1			

Week 9:

16 Weeks
to race day

**BASE
PHASE 3**

Monday	Tuesday	Wednesday
Technique swim	**Bike (AM) strength set**	**Swim – intensity set**
Warm-up 300m easy Z1 freestyle	*This set is best completed on a hill or, if a hill is unavailable, a stationary bike trainer.*	*Warm-up* 400m easy freestyle and backstroke – 75m freestyle, 25m backstroke
200m freestyle – 75m Z2, 25m easy Z1	*Warm-up* 10 minutes Z1	200m freestyle – 25m hard, 25m easy
100m steady Z2 freestyle	4 x 1-minute hard efforts on a 1-minute Z2 recovery	200m easy Z2 freestyle
Main set 10 x 50m as: 25m drill-of-choice 1 into 25m freestyle	2 minutes Z2	*Main set* 10 x 250m freestyle on a 10-second RI as:
300m Z1 freestyle	*Main set* 4 x 6 minutes Z2 low cadence (70-80 RPM) on an easy downhill recovery back to your start position and repeat	4 x 250m easy Z2 3 x 250m tempo Z3 2 x 250m threshold Z4 1 x 250m threshold+ Z5a
10 x 50m as: 25m drill-of-choice 2 into 25 freestyle	1 x 10 minutes Z3 on an easy downhill recovery back to your starting point	*Cool down* 500m easy freestyle and backstroke – 75m freestyle, 25m backstroke
300m Z1 freestyle	20 minutes Z2	**Bike – just-for-fun (PM)**
Cool down 200m Z1 freestyle	*Cool down* 10 minutes easy Z1 spin	70 minutes easy
	Run – just-for-fun (PM)	
	50 minutes easy	

Thursday	Friday	Saturday	Sunday
Bike (AM) – strength/ intensity set	**Swim – long/ strength**	**Long ride**	**Long run**
This set is best completed on a hill or, if a hill is unavailable, a stationary bike trainer.	*Warm-up* 400m easy freestyle and backstroke – 75m freestyle, 25m backstroke	4 hrs 30 mins	140 minutes
Warm-up 10 minutes Z1		*Warm-up* 10 minutes Z1	*Warm-up* 10 minutes Z1
4 x 1-minute hard efforts on a 1-minute Z2 recovery	300m easy Z1 freestyle	*Main set* 4hrs 15 mins: target Z1/2	10 minutes building to Z2
2 minutes Z2	200m freestyle – 75m Z2, 25m easy Z1	Try to include a 30-minute Z3 effort.	*Main set* 115 minutes Z2
Main set **6 x 6 minutes odd/ even** Odd (reps 1,3,5): Z2 low cadence (70-80 RPM) Even (reps 2,4,6): Z3 cadence (85-90+)	100m steady Z2 freestyle	*Cool down* 5 minutes easy Z1 spinning	Include walk breaks when necessary. A couple of minutes every 20-60 minutes is recommended.
All on an easy downhill recovery (2.5-3 minute spin) back to your start position and repeat	*Main set* 9 x 200m Z2 on a 10-second RI as: 1. Freestyle swim 2. Freestyle with paddles 3. Freestyle with paddles and pull buoy		*Cool down* 5 minutes easy Z1 running
20 minutes Z2			
Cool down 10 minutes easy Z1 spin			
Run – interval set *Warm-up* 10 minutes Z1	Repeat for a total of 3 sets.		
4 x 1-minute hard (Z4)	*Cool down* 500m easy freestyle and backstroke – 75m freestyle, 25m backstroke		
1 minute easy (Z2)			
2 minutes Z2			
Main set 5 x 5 minutes Z4 on a 30-second easy Z1 recovery jog			
Cool down 10 minutes Z1			

Week 10:

**15 Weeks
to race day**

**BASE
PHASE 3**

Monday	Tuesday	Wednesday
Technique swim	**Bike (AM) strength set**	**Swim – intensity set**

Monday

Technique swim

Warm-up
300m easy Z1 freestyle

200m freestyle –
75m Z2, 25m easy Z1

100m steady Z2
freestyle

Main set
10 x 50m as:
25m drill-of-choice 1 into
25m freestyle

300m Z1 freestyle

10 x 50m as:
25m drill-of-choice 2 into
25 freestyle

300m Z1 freestyle

Cool down
200m Z1 freestyle

Tuesday

Bike (AM) strength set

*This set is best
completed on a hill or,
if a hill is unavailable, a
stationary bike trainer.*

Warm-up
10 minutes Z1

4 x 1-minute hard efforts
on a 1-minute

Z2 recovery

2 minutes Z2

Main set
4 x 6 minutes Z2 low
cadence (70-80 RPM)
on an easy downhill
recovery back to your
start position and repeat

1 x 10 minutes Z3
on an easy downhill
recovery back to your
starting point

20 minutes Z2

Cool down
10 minutes easy Z1 spin

Run – just-for-fun (PM)

50 minutes easy

Wednesday

Swim – intensity set

Warm-up
400m easy freestyle
and backstroke –
75m freestyle,
25m backstroke

200m freestyle –
25m hard, 25m easy

200m easy Z2 freestyle

Main set
10 x 250m freestyle on a
10-second RI as:
4 x 250m easy Z2
3 x 50m tempo Z3
2 x 250m threshold Z4
1 x 250m threshold+ Z5a

Cool down
500m easy freestyle
and backstroke –
75m freestyle,
25m backstroke

Bike – just-for-fun (PM)

70 minutes easy

Thursday	Friday	Saturday	Sunday
Bike (AM) – strength/ intensity set	**Swim – long/ strength**	**Long ride**	**Long run**
This set is best completed on a hill or, if a hill is unavailable, a stationary bike trainer.		5 hours	140 minutes
	Warm-up 400m easy freestyle and backstroke – 75m freestyle, 25m backstroke	*Warm-up* 10 minutes Z1	*Warm-up* 10 minutes Z1
Warm-up 10 minutes Z1		*Main set* 4 hrs 45 mins: target Z1/2	10 minutes building to Z2
4 x 1-minute hard efforts on a 1-minute Z2 recovery	300m easy Z1 freestyle	Try to include a 30-minute Z3 effort.	*Main set* 105 minutes Z2
2 minutes Z2	200m freestyle – 75m Z2, 25m easy Z1	*Cool down* 5 minutes easy Z1 spinning	Include walk breaks when necessary. A couple of minutes every 20-60 minutes is recommended.
Main set **6 x 6 minutes odd/ even** Odd (reps 1,3,5): Z2 low cadence (70-80 RPM) Even (reps 2,4,6): Z3 cadence (85-90+)	100m steady Z2 freestyle *Main set* 9 x 200m Z2 on a 10-second RI as:		*Cool down* 5 minutes easy Z1 running
All on an easy downhill recovery (2.5-3 minute spin) back to your start position and repeat	1. Freestyle swim 2. Freestyle with pull buoy 3. Freestyle with pull buoy and paddles		
20 minutes Z2	Repeat for a total of 3 sets.		
Cool down 10 minutes easy Z1 spin	*Cool down* 500m easy freestyle and backstroke – 75m freestyle, 25m backstroke		
Run – interval set			
Warm-up 10 minutes Z1			
4 x 1-minute hard (Z4)			
1 minute easy (Z2)			
2 minutes Z2			
Main set 5 x 5 minutes Z4 on a 30-second easy Z1 recovery jog			
Cool down 10 minutes Z1			

Week 11:

14 Weeks
to race day

**BASE
PHASE 3**

Monday	Tuesday	Wednesday
Technique swim	**Bike (AM) strength set**	**Swim – intensity set**
Warm-up 300m easy Z1 freestyle	*This set is best completed on a hill or, if a hill is unavailable, a stationary bike trainer.*	*Warm-up* 400m easy freestyle and backstroke – 75m freestyle, 25m backstroke
200m freestyle – 75m Z2, 25m easy Z1	*Warm-up* 10 minutes Z1	200m freestyle – 25m hard, 25m easy
100m steady Z2 freestyle	4 x 1-minute hard efforts on a 1-minute Z2 recovery	200m easy Z2 freestyle
Main set 10 x 50m as: 25m drill-of-choice 1 into 25m freestyle	2 minutes Z2	*Main set* 10 x 300m freestyle on a 10-second RI as:
300m Z1 freestyle	*Main set* 4 x 6 minutes Z2 low cadence (70-80 RPM) on an easy downhill recovery back to your start position and repeat	4 x 300m easy Z2 3 x 300m tempo Z3 2 x 300m threshold Z4 1 x 300m threshold+ Z5a
10 x 50m as: 25m drill-of-choice 2 into 25 freestyle		*Cool down* 500m easy freestyle and backstroke – 75m freestyle, 25m backstroke
300m Z1 freestyle	1 x 10 minutes Z3 on an easy downhill recovery back to your starting point	
Cool down 200m Z1 freestyle	20 minutes Z2	**Bike – Just-for-fun (PM)**
	Cool down 10 minutes easy Z1 spin	80 minutes easy
	Run – just-for-fun (PM)	
	50 minutes easy	

Thursday	Friday	Saturday	Sunday
Bike (AM) – strength/intensity set	**Swim – long/strength**	**Long run**	**Long ride**
This set is best completed on a hill or, if a hill is unavailable, a stationary bike trainer.	*Warm-up*	150 minutes	5 hours
	400m easy freestyle and backstroke – 75m freestyle, 25m backstroke	*Warm-up* 10 minutes Z1	*Warm-up* 10 minutes Z1
Warm-up 10 minutes Z1		10 minutes building to Z2	*Main set* 4hrs 45 mins: target Z1/2
4 x 1-minute hard efforts on a 1-minute Z2 recovery	300m easy Z1 freestyle	*Main set* 115 minutes Z2	Try to include a 30-minute Z3 effort.
2 minutes Z2	200m freestyle – 75m Z2, 25m easy Z1	Include walk breaks when necessary. A couple of minutes every 20-60 minutes is recommended.	*Cool down* 5 minutes easy Z1 spinning
Main set **6 x 6 minutes odd/even** Odd (reps 1, 3,5): Z2 low cadence (70-80 RPM) Even (reps 2,4,6): Z3 cadence (85-90+)	100m steady Z2 freestyle		
	Main set 9 x 200m Z2 on a 10-second RI as:	*Cool down* 5 minutes easy Z1 running	
All on an easy downhill recovery (2.5-3-minute spin) back to your start position and repeat	1. Freestyle swim 2. Freestyle with pull buoy 3. Freestyle with pull buoy and paddles		
20 minutes Z2			
Cool down 10 minutes easy Z1 spin	Repeat for a total of 3 sets.		
Run – tempo *Warm-up* 10 minutes Z1	*Cool down* 500m easy freestyle and backstroke – 75m freestyle, 25m backstroke		
15 minutes Z2			
Main set 2 x 15 minutes Z3 on an easy 2-minute Z2 recovery			
Cool down 5 minutes Z1			

Week 12:

13 Weeks
to race day

**BASE
PHASE 3**

Monday	Tuesday	Wednesday
Day off	**Recovery swim or just-for-fun bike**	**Bike (AM) – strength set**
		This set is best completed on a hill or, if a hill is unavailable, a stationary bike trainer.
	Swim Easy 40-50 minute Z1 freestyle	*Warm-up* 10 minutes Z1
	Or	4 x 1-minute hard efforts on a 1-minute Z2 recovery
	Bike Easy 50-60 minute Z1 spin	2 minutes Z2
		Main set 4 x 6 minutes Z2 low cadence (70-80 RPM) on an easy downhill recovery back to your start position and repeat
		1 x 10 minutes Z3 on an easy downhill recovery back to your starting point
		20 minutes Z2
		Cool down 10 minutes easy Z1 spin

Thursday	Friday	Saturday	Sunday
Bike (AM) – strength/ intensity set	**Swim – long/ strength**	**Long ride**	**Long run**
This set is best completed on a hill or, if a hill is unavailable, a stationary bike trainer.	*Warm-up* 400m easy freestyle and backstroke – 75m freestyle, 25m backstroke	5 hours *Warm-up* 10 minutes Z1	150 minutes *Warm-up* 10 minutes Z1
Warm-up 10 minutes Z1	300m easy Z1 freestyle	*Main set* 4hrs 45 mins: target Z1/2	10 minutes building to Z2
4 x 1-minute hard efforts on a 1-minute Z2 recovery	200m freestyle – 75m Z2, 25m easy Z1	Try to include 2 x 30-minute Z3 efforts.	*Main set* 105 minutes Z2
2 minutes Z2	100m steady Z2 freestyle	*Cool down* 5 minutes easy Z1 spinning	Include walk breaks when necessary. A couple of minutes every 20-60 minutes is recommended.
Main set **6 x 6 minutes odd/ even** Odd (reps 1, 3,5): Z2 low cadence (70-80 RPM) Even (reps 2,4,6): Z3 cadence (85-90+)	*Main set* 9 x 200m Z2 on a 10-second RI as:		*Cool down* 5 minutes easy Z1 running
All on an easy downhill recovery (2.5-3 minute spin) back to your start position and repeat	1. Freestyle swim 2. Freestyle with pull buoy 3. Freestyle with pull buoy and paddles		
20 minutes Z2	Repeat for a total of 3 sets.		
Cool down 10 minutes easy Z1 spin	*Cool down* 500m easy freestyle and backstroke – 75m freestyle, 25m backstroke		
Run – tempo			
Warm-up 10 minutes Z1			
10 minutes Z2			
Main set 2 x 8 minutes Z3 on an easy 5-minute Z2 recovery			
Cool down 5 minutes Z1			

Week 13:

12 Weeks
to race day

**BUILD
PHASE 1**

Monday	Tuesday	Wednesday
Technique swim	**Bike (AM) strength set**	**Swim – intensity set**
Warm-up 300m easy Z1 freestyle	*This set is best completed on a hill or, if a hill is unavailable, a stationary bike trainer.*	*Warm-up* 400m easy freestyle and backstroke – 75m freestyle, 25m backstroke
200m freestyle – 75m Z2, 25m easy Z1	*Warm-up* 10 minutes Z1	
100m steady Z2 freestyle	4 x 1-minute hard efforts on a 1-minute Z2 recovery	200m freestyle – 25m hard, 25m easy
Main set 10 x 50m as: 25m drill-of-choice 1 into 25m freestyle	2 minutes Z2	200m easy Z2 freestyle
	Main set 2 x 6 minutes Z2 low cadence (70-80 RPM) on an easy downhill recovery back to your start position and repeat	*Main set* 10 x 300m freestyle on a 10-second RI as: 4 x 300m easy Z2 3 x 300m tempo Z3 2 x 300m threshold Z4 1 x 300m threshold+ Z5a
300m Z1 freestyle		
10 x 50m as: 25m drill-of-choice 2 into 25 freestyle		
300m Z1 freestyle	2 x 10 minutes Z3 on an easy downhill recovery back to your starting point	*Cool down* 500m easy freestyle and backstroke – 75m freestyle, 25m backstroke
Cool down 200m Z1 freestyle	20 minutes Z2	**Bike – just-for-fun (PM)**
	Cool down 10 minutes easy Z1 spin	80 minutes easy
	Run – just-for-fun (PM)	
	60 minutes easy	

Thursday	Friday	Saturday	Sunday
Bike (AM) – intensity set	**Swim – long/ strength**	**Long ride**	**Long run**
This set is best completed on a hill or, if a hill is unavailable, a stationary bike trainer.	*Warm-up* 400m easy freestyle and backstroke – 75m freestyle, 25m backstroke	5 hrs 30 mins	150 minutes
Warm-up 10 minutes Z1	300m easy Z1 freestyle	*Warm-up* 10 minutes Z1	*Warm-up* 10 minutes Z1
4 x 1-minute hard efforts on a 1-minute Z2 recovery	200m freestyle – 75m Z2, 25m easy Z1	*Main set* 5hrs 15 mins: target Z1/2	10 minutes building to Z2
2 minutes Z2	100m steady Z2 freestyle	Try to include 2 x 30-minute Z3 efforts.	*Main set* 105 minutes Z2
Main set 3 x 10 minutes Z3 on an easy 4-5 minute downhill spin	*Main set* 8 x 250m Z2 on a 10-second RI as:	*Cool down* 5 minutes easy Z1 spinning	Include walk breaks when necessary. A couple of minutes every 20-60 minutes is recommended.
20 minutes Z2	1. Freestyle swim		*Cool down* 5 minutes easy Z1 running
Cool down 10 minutes easy Z1 spin	2. Freestyle with paddles		
Run – interval set	3. Freestyle with paddles and pull Buoy		
Warm-up 10 minutes Z1	4. Freestyle with paddles, pull buoy and band		
4 x 1-minute hard (Z4)	Repeat for a total of 2 sets.		
1 minute easy (Z2)	*Cool down* 500m easy freestyle and backstroke – 75m freestyle, 25m backstroke		
2 minutes Z2			
Main set 5 x 6 minutes Z4 on a 30-second easy Z1 recovery Jog			
Cool down 10 minutes Z1			

Week 14:

11 Weeks
to race day

**BUILD
PHASE 1**

Monday	Tuesday	Wednesday
Technique swim	**Brick (AM)**	**Swim – intensity set**

Monday

Technique swim

Warm-up
300m easy Z1 freestyle

200m freestyle – 75m
Z2, 25m easy Z1

100m steady Z2
freestyle

Main set
10 x 50m as: 25m drill-
of-choice 1 into 25m
freestyle

300m Z1 freestyle

10 x 50m as: 25m
drill-of-choice 2 into 25
freestyle

300m Z1 freestyle

Cool down
200m Z1 freestyle

Tuesday

Brick (AM)

This set is best
completed on a hill or,
if a hill is unavailable, a
stationary bike trainer.

Warm-up
10 minutes Z1

4 x 1-minute hard
efforts on a 1-minute Z2
recovery

2 minutes Z2

Main set
4 x 6 minutes Z2 low
cadence (70-80 RPM)
on an easy downhill
recovery back to your
start position and repeat

1 x 10 minutes Z3
on an easy downhill
recovery back to your
starting point

10 minutes Z2

Run off the bike
10 minutes IMRP
(Ironman race pace)

Cool down
5-10 minutes Z1

Run – just-for-fun (PM)

60 minutes easy

Wednesday

Swim – intensity set

Warm-up
400m easy freestyle
and backstroke –
75m freestyle,
25m backstroke

200m freestyle –
25m hard, 25m easy

200m easy Z2 freestyle

Main set
10 x 300m freestyle on a
10-second RI as:
4 x 300m easy Z2
3 x 300m tempo Z3
2 x 300m threshold Z4
1 x 300m threshold+ Z5a

Cool down
500m easy freestyle
and backstroke –
75m freestyle,
25m backstroke

Bike – just-for-fun (PM)

80 minutes easy

Thursday	Friday	Saturday	Sunday
Bike (AM) – intensity set	**Swim – long/ strength**	**Long ride**	**Long run**
This set is best completed on a hill or, if a hill is unavailable, a stationary bike trainer.	*Warm-up* 400m easy freestyle and backstroke – 75m freestyle, 25m backstroke	5 hrs 30 mins	150 minutes
		Warm-up 10 minutes Z1	*Warm-up* 10 minutes Z1
Warm-up 10 minutes Z1	300m easy Z1 freestyle	*Main set* 5hrs 15 mins: target Z1/2	10 minutes building to Z2
4 x 1-minute hard efforts on a 1-minute Z2 recovery	200m freestyle – 75m Z2, 25m easy Z1	Try to include 2 x 30-minute Z3 efforts.	*Main set* 105 minutes Z2
2 minutes Z2	100m steady Z2 freestyle	*Cool down* 5 minutes easy Z1 spinning	Include walk breaks when necessary. A couple of minutes every 20-60 minutes is recommended.
Main set 3 x 10 minutes Z3 on an easy 4-5 minute downhill spin	*Main set* 8 x 250m Z2 on a 10-second RI as:		*Cool down* 5 minutes easy Z1 running
20 minutes Z2	1. Freestyle swim		
Cool down 10 minutes easy Z1 spin	2. Freestyle with paddles		
	3. Freestyle with paddles and pull buoy		
Run – tempo	4. Freestyle with paddles, pull buoy and band		
Warm-up 10 minutes Z1	Repeat for a total of 2 sets.		
10 minutes Z2	*Cool down* 500m easy freestyle and backstroke – 75m freestyle, 25m backstroke		
Main set 10 minutes Z2			
30 minutes Z3			
Cool down 5 minutes Z1			

Week 15:

10 Weeks
to race day

BUILD
PHASE 1

Monday	Tuesday	Wednesday
Technique swim	**Brick (AM)**	**Swim – intensity set**
Warm-up 300m easy Z1 freestyle	*This set is best completed on a hill or, if a hill is unavailable, a stationary bike trainer.*	*Warm-up* 400m easy freestyle and backstroke – 75m freestyle, 25m backstroke
200m freestyle – 75m Z2, 25m easy Z1	*Warm-up* 10 minutes Z1	
100m steady Z2 freestyle	4 x 1-minute hard efforts on a 1-minute Z2 recovery	200m freestyle – 25m hard, 25m easy
Main set 10 x 50m as: 25m drill-of-choice 1 into 25m freestyle	2 minutes Z2	200m easy Z2 freestyle
	Main set 4 x 6 minutes Z2 low cadence (70-80 RPM) on an easy downhill recovery back to your start position and repeat	*Main set* 10 x 300m freestyle on a 10-second RI completed as:
300m Z1 freestyle		4 x 300m easy Z2 3 x 300m tempo Z3 2 x 300m threshold Z4 1 x 300m threshold+ Z5a
10 x 50m as: 25m drill-of-choice 2 into 25 freestyle		
300m Z1 freestyle	1 x 10 minutes Z3 on an easy downhill recovery back to your starting point	*Cool down* 500m easy freestyle and backstroke – 75m freestyle, 25m backstroke
Cool down 200m Z1 freestyle	10 minutes Z2	
	Run off the bike 10 minutes IMRP	**Bike – just-for-fun (PM)**
	Cool down 5-10 minutes Z1	80 minutes easy
	Run – just-for-fun (PM)	
	60minutes easy	

Thursday	Friday	Saturday	Sunday
Bike (AM) – intensity set *This set is best completed on a hill or, if a hill is unavailable, a stationary bike trainer.* *Warm-up* 10 minutes Z1 4 x 1-minute hard efforts on a 1-minute Z2 recovery 2 minutes Z2 *Main set* 3 x 10 minutes Z3 on an easy 4-5 minute downhill spin 20 minutes Z2 *Cool down* 10 minutes easy Z1 spin **Run – long interval set** *Warm-up* 10 minutes Z1 4 x 1-minute hard (Z4) 1 minute easy (Z2) 2 minutes Z2 *Main set* 1 x 10 minutes Z3 on a 30-second easy Z1 recovery jog 2 x 10 minutes Z4 on an easy 2-minute Z1 recovery jog *Cool down* 10 minutes Z1	**Swim – long/ strength** *Warm-up* 400m easy freestyle and backstroke – 75m freestyle, 25m backstroke 300m easy Z1 freestyle 200m freestyle – 75m Z2, 25m easy Z1 100m steady Z2 freestyle *Main set* 8 x 250m Z2 on a 10-second RI as: 1. Freestyle swim 2. Freestyle with paddles 3. Freestyle with paddles and pull buoy 4. Freestyle with paddles, pull buoy and band Repeat for a total of 2 sets. *Cool down* 500m easy freestyle and backstroke – 75m freestyle, 25m backstroke	**Long run** 160 minutes *Warm-up* 10 minutes Z1 10 minutes building to Z2 *Main set* 135 minutes Z2 Include walk breaks when necessary. A couple of minutes every 20-60 minutes is recommended. *Cool down* 5 minutes easy Z1 running	**Long ride** 5 hrs 30 mins *Warm-up* 10 minutes Z1 *Main set* 5hrs 15 mins: target Z1/2 Try to include 6 x 20-minute efforts at IMRP (Ironman race pace) on a 5-10 minute easy spin. *Cool down* 5 minutes easy Z1 spinning

Week 16:

9 Weeks to race day

BUILD PHASE 1

Monday	Tuesday	Wednesday
Day off	**Recovery swim or just-for-fun bike**	**Bike (AM) – strength set**

Tuesday

Recovery swim or just-for-fun bike

Swim
Easy 40-50 minute Z1 freestyle

Or

Bike
Easy 50-60 minute Z1 spin

Wednesday

Bike (AM) – strength set
This set is best completed on a hill or, if a hill is unavailable, a stationary bike trainer.

Warm-up
10 minutes Z1

4 x 1-minute hard efforts on a 1-minute Z2 recovery

2 minutes Z2

Main set
4 x 6 minutes Z2 low cadence (70-80 RPM) on an easy downhill recovery back to your start position and repeat

1 x 10 minutes Z3 on an easy downhill recovery back to your starting point

20 minutes Z2

Cool down
10 minutes easy Z1 spin

Thursday	Friday	Saturday	Sunday
Bike (AM) – intensity set	**Swim – long/ strength**	**Long ride**	**Recovery bike**
This set is best completed on the flat or a stationary bike trainer.	*Warm-up* 400m easy freestyle and backstroke – 75m freestyle, 25m backstroke	6-7 hours (ideally aim to cover 180-200km)	30-minute easy Z1 spin
Warm-up 10 minute Z1	300m easy Z1 freestyle	*Warm-up* 10 minutes Z1	**Long run** 100 minutes
4 x 1-minute hard efforts on a 1-minute Z2 recovery	200m freestyle – 75m Z2, 25m easy Z1	*Main set* 5 hrs 45 mins – 6 hrs 45 mins: target Z1/2	*Warm-up* 10 minutes Z1
2 minutes Z2	100m steady Z2 freestyle	*Cool down* 5 minutes easy Z1 spinning	10 minutes building to Z2
Main set 1 x 10 minutes Z3 on an easy 2-minute spin	*Main set* 8 x 250m Z2 on a 10-second RI as:		*Main set* 75 minutes Z2
2 x 15 minutes Z3 on an easy 3-4 minute spin	1. Freestyle swim 2. Freestyle with paddles		Include walk breaks when necessary. A couple of minutes every 20-60 minutes is recommended.
Cool down 10 minutes easy Z1 spin	3. Freestyle with paddles and pull buoy 4. Freestyle with paddles, pull buoy and band		*Cool down* 5 minutes easy Z1 running
Run – tempo	Repeat for a total of 2 sets.		
Warm-up 10 minutes Z1	*Cool down* 500m easy freestyle and backstroke – 75m freestyle, 25m backstroke		
10 minutes Z2			
Main set 2 x 8 minutes Z3 on an easy 5-minute Z2 recovery			
Cool down 5 minutes Z1			

Week 17:

8 Weeks
to race day

**BUILD
PHASE 2**

Monday	Tuesday	Wednesday
Technique swim	**Brick (AM)**	**Swim – intensity set**
Warm-up 300m easy Z1 freestyle	*This set is best completed on a hill or, if a hill is unavailable, a stationary bike trainer.*	*Warm-up* 200m easy freestyle and backstroke – 75m freestyle, 25m backstroke
200m freestyle – 75m Z2, 25m easy Z1	*Warm-up* 10 minutes Z1	200m freestyle – 25m hard, 25m easy
100m steady Z2 freestyle	4 x 1-minute hard efforts on a 1-minute Z2 recovery	*Main set* 10 x 350m freestyle on a 10-second RI completed as:
Main set 10 x 50m as: 25m drill-of-choice 1 into 25m freestyle	2 minutes Z2	4 x 350m easy Z2 3 x 350m tempo Z3 2 x 350m threshold Z4 1 x 350m threshold+ Z5a
300m Z1 freestyle	*Main set* 4 x 10 minutes Z3 on an easy (5-minute) downhill recovery spin back to your starting point and repeat	*Cool down* 500m easy freestyle and backstroke – 75m freestyle, 25m backstroke
10 x 50m as: 25m drill-of-choice 2 into 25 freestyle	10 minutes Z2	**Bike – just-for-fun (PM)**
300m Z1 freestyle	*Run off the bike* 10 minutes IMRP	80 minutes easy
Cool down 200m Z1 freestyle	*Cool down* 5-10 minutes Z1	
	Run – just-for-fun (PM)	
	70 minutes easy	

Thursday	Friday	Saturday	Sunday
Bike (AM) – intensity set	**Swim – long/ strength**	**Long ride**	**Long run**
This set is best completed on the flat or a stationary bike trainer.		5 hours	170 minutes
	Warm-up	*Warm-up*	*Warm-up*
	400m easy freestyle and backstroke – 75m freestyle, 25m backstroke	10 minutes Z1	10 minutes Z1
Warm-up		10 minutes building to Z2	10 minutes building to Z2
10 minute Z1			
	300m easy Z1 freestyle	60 minutes Z2	*Main set*
4 x 1-minute hard efforts on a 1-minute Z2 recovery			145 minutes Z2
		Main set	
2 minutes Z2	200m freestyle – 75m Z2, 25m easy Z1	1 x 20-minute 3 x 30-minute 1 x 20-minute efforts at IMRP on a 5-10 minute easy Z1/2 spin	Include walk breaks when necessary. A couple of minutes every 20-60 minutes is recommended.
Main set			
1 x 10 minutes Z3 on an easy 2-minute spin	100m steady Z2 freestyle		
2 x 15 minutes Z3 on an easy 3-4 minute spin	*Main set*		*Cool down*
	8 x 250m Z2 on a 10-second RI as:	*Run off the bike*	5 minutes easy Z1 running
Cool down		15 minutes IMRP	
10 minutes easy Z1 spin	1. Freestyle swim		
	2. Freestyle with paddles	*Cool down*	
Run – long interval set	3. Freestyle with paddles and pull buoy	5-10 minutes Z1	
Warm-up	4. Freestyle with paddles, pull buoy and band		
10 minutes Z1			
4 x 1-minute hard (Z4)	Repeat for a total of 2 sets.		
1 minute easy (Z2)	*Cool down*		
2 minutes Z2	500m easy freestyle and backstroke – 75m freestyle, 25m backstroke		
Main set			
1 x 10 minutes Z3 on a 30-second easy Z1 recovery jog			
2 x 10 minutes Z4 on an easy 2-minute Z1 recovery jog			
Cool down			
10 minutes Z1			

Week 18:

7 Weeks
to race day

**BUILD
PHASE 2**

Monday	Tuesday	Wednesday
Technique swim	**Brick (AM)**	**Swim – intensity set**
Warm-up 300m easy Z1 freestyle	*This set is best completed on a hill or, if a hill is unavailable, a stationary bike trainer.*	*Warm-up* 400m easy freestyle and backstroke – 75m freestyle, 25m backstroke
200m freestyle – 75m Z2, 25m easy Z1	*Warm-up* 10 minutes Z1	200m freestyle – 25m hard, 25m easy
100m steady Z2 freestyle	4 x 1-minute hard efforts on a 1-minute Z2 recovery	*Main set* 10 x 350m freestyle on a 10-second RI as:
Main set 10 x 50m as: 25m drill-of-choice 1 into 25m freestyle	2 minutes Z2	4 x 350m easy Z2 3 x 350m tempo Z3 2 x 350m threshold Z4 1 x 350m threshold+ Z5a
300m Z1 freestyle	*Main set* 4 x 10 minute Z3 on an easy (5-minute) downhill recovery spin back to your starting point and repeat	*Cool down* 500m easy freestyle and backstroke – 75m freestyle, 25m backstroke
10 x 50m as: 25m drill-of-choice 2 into 25m freestyle	10 minutes Z2	**Bike – just-for-fun (PM)**
300m Z1 freestyle	*Run off the bike* 10 minutes IMRP	80 minutes easy
Cool down 200m Z1 freestyle	*Cool down* 5-10 minutes Z1	
	Run – just-for-fun (PM)	
	70 minutes easy	

Thursday	Friday	Saturday	Sunday
Bike (AM) – intensity set	**Swim – long/ strength**	**Long ride**	**Long run**
This set is best completed on the flat or a stationary bike trainer.		5 hours	180 minutes
	Warm-up	*Warm-up*	*Warm-up*
Warm-up	400m easy freestyle and backstroke –	10 minutes Z1	10 minutes Z1
10 minutes Z1	75m freestyle, 25m backstroke	10 minutes building to Z2	10 minutes building to Z2
4 x 1-minute hard efforts on a 1-minute Z2 recovery	300m easy Z1 freestyle	60 minutes Z2	*Main set* 155 minutes Z2
2 minutes Z2	200m freestyle – 75m Z2, 25m easy Z1	*Main set* 1 x 15-minute 5 x 30-minute 1 x 15-minute efforts at IMRP on a 5-10 minute easy Z1/2 spin	Include walk breaks when necessary. A couple of minutes every 20-60 minutes is recommended.
Main set 1 x 10 minutes Z3 on an easy 2-3 minute spin	100m steady Z2 freestyle		
1 x 20 minutes Z3 on an easy 3-4 minute spin	*Main set* 8 x 300m Z2 on a 10-second RI as:	*Run off the bike* 20 minutes IMRP	*Cool down* 5 minutes easy Z1 running
1 x 10 minutes Z3 on an easy 2-3 minute spin	1. Freestyle swim	*Cool down* 5-10 minutes Z1	
Cool down 10 minutes easy Z1 spin	2. Freestyle with Paddles		
Run – long interval set *Warm-up* 10 minutes Z1	3. Freestyle with paddles and pull buoy		
4 x 1-minute hard (Z4)	4. Freestyle with paddles, pull buoy and band		
1 minute easy (Z2)			
2 minutes Z2	Repeat for a total of 2 sets.		
Main set 1 x 10 minutes Z3 on a 30-second easy Z1 recovery jog	*Cool down* 500m easy freestyle and backstroke –		
2 x 10 minutes Z4 on an easy 2-minute Z1 recovery jog	75m freestyle, 25m backstroke		
Cool down 10 minutes Z1			

Week 19:

6 Weeks to race day

BUILD PHASE 2

Monday	Tuesday	Wednesday
Technique swim	**Brick (AM)**	**Swim – intensity set**
Warm-up 300m easy Z1 freestyle	*This set is best completed on a hill or, if a hill is unavailable, a stationary bike trainer.*	*Warm-up* 400m easy freestyle and backstroke – 75m freestyle, 25m backstroke
200m freestyle – 75m Z2, 25m easy Z1	*Warm-up* 10 minutes Z1	
100m steady Z2 freestyle	4 x 1-minute hard efforts on a 1-minute Z2 recovery	200m freestyle – 25m hard, 25m easy
Main set 10 x 50m as: 25m drill-of-choice 1 into 25m freestyle	2 minutes Z2	*Main set* 10 x 350m freestyle on a 10-second RI completed as:
300m Z1 freestyle	*Main set* 4 x 10 minutes Z3 on an easy (5-minute) downhill recovery spin back to your starting point and repeat	4 x 350m easy Z2 3 x 350m tempo Z3 2 x 350m threshold Z4 1 x 350m threshold+ Z5a
10 x 50m as: 25m drill-of-choice 2 into 25 freestyle	10 minutes Z2	*Cool down* 500m easy freestyle and backstroke – 75m freestyle, 25m backstroke
300m Z1 freestyle	*Run off the bike* 10 minutes IMRP	
Cool down 200m Z1 freestyle	*Cool down* 5-10 minutes Z1	**Bike – just-for-fun (PM)**
	Run – just-for-fun (PM)	80 minutes easy
	70 minutes easy	

Thursday	Friday	Saturday	Sunday
Bike (AM) – intensity set	**Swim – long/ strength**	**Race simulation**	**Day off**
This set is best completed on the flat or a stationary bike trainer.	*Warm-up* 400m easy freestyle and backstroke – 75m freestyle, 25m backstroke	*Warm-up* 10 minutes easy Z1 swim	or Easy 30-minute recovery bike
Warm-up 10 minutes Z1		Race simulation at Ironman intensity: 45-minute swim 4-hour bike 2-hour run	
4 x 1-minute hard efforts on a 1-minute Z2 recovery	300m easy Z1 freestyle		
	200m freestyle – 75m Z2, 25m easy Z1	*Cool down* Keep the last 10 minutes of the run easy.	
2 minutes Z2	100m steady Z2 freestyle		
Main set 1 x 10 minutes Z3 on an easy 2-3 minute spin	*Main set* 8 x 300m Z2 on a 10-second RI as:		
1 x 20 minutes Z3 on an easy 3-4 minute spin	1. Freestyle swim 2. Freestyle with paddles		
1 x 10 minutes Z3 on an easy 2-3 minute spin	3. Freestyle with paddles and pull buoy		
Cool down 10 minutes easy Z1 spin	4. Freestyle with paddles, pull buoy and band		
Run – build run	Repeat for a total of 2 sets.		
Warm-up 10 minutes Z1	*Cool down* 500m easy freestyle and backstroke – 75m freestyle, 25m backstroke		
10 minutes Z2			
Main set 10 minutes Z2			
20 minutes Z3			
Cool down 5 minutes Z1			

Week 20:

5 Weeks
to race day

**BUILD
PHASE 2**

Recovery
Week

Monday	Tuesday	Wednesday
Day off	**Recovery swim or just-for-fun bike**	**Bike (AM) – intensity set**

Tuesday

Recovery swim or just-for-fun bike

Swim
Easy 40-50 minute Z1 freestyle

Or

Bike
Easy 50-60 minute Z1 spin

Wednesday

Bike (AM) – intensity set

This set is best completed on a hill or, if a hill is unavailable, a stationary bike trainer.

Warm-up
10 minutes Z1

4 x 1-minute hard efforts on a 1-minute   Z2 recovery

2 minutes Z2

Main set

4 x 10 minutes Z3 on an easy (5-minute) downhill recovery spin back to your starting point and repeat

20 minutes Z2

Cool down
10 minutes easy Z1 spin

Thursday	Friday	Saturday	Sunday
Bike (AM) – intensity set	**Swim – long/ strength**	**Long ride**	**Long run**
This set is best completed on the flat or a stationary bike trainer.	*Warm-up* 400m easy freestyle and backstroke – 75m freestyle, 25m backstroke	5 hours	180 minutes
Warm-up 10 minutes Z1		*Warm-up* 10 minutes Z1	*Warm-up* 10 minutes Z1
		10 minutes building to Z2	10 minutes building to Z2
4 x 1-minute hard efforts on a 1-minute Z2 recovery	300m easy Z1 freestyle	60 minutes Z2	*Main set* 155 minutes Z2
2 minutes Z2	200m freestyle – 75m Z2, 25m easy Z1	*Main set* 1 x 15-minute 5 x 30-minute 1 x 15-minute efforts at IMRP on a 5-10 minute easy Z1/2 spin	Include walk breaks when necessary. A couple of minutes every 20-60 minutes is recommended.
Main set 2 x 20 minutes Z3 on an easy 3-4 minute spin	100m steady Z2 freestyle		
	Main set 8 x 300m Z2 on a 10-second RI as:		
Cool down 10 minutes easy		*Cool down* 5 minutes easy Z1 spinning	*Cool down* 5 minutes easy Z1 running
Z1 spin	1. Freestyle swim 2. Freestyle with paddles		
Run – tempo	3. Freestyle with paddles and pull buoy		
Warm-up 10 minutes Z1	4. Freestyle with paddles, pull buoy and band		
10 minutes Z2			
Main set 2 x 8 minutes Z3 on an easy 5-minute Z2 recovery	Repeat for a total of 2 sets.		
Cool down 5 minutes Z1	*Cool down* 500m easy freestyle and backstroke – 75m freestyle, 25m backstroke		

Week 21:

4 Weeks to race day

PEAK WEEK

Monday	Tuesday	Wednesday
Technique swim	**Bike (AM) – intensity set**	**Swim – intensity set**
Warm-up 300m easy Z1 freestyle	*This set is best completed on a hill or, if a hill is unavailable, a stationary bike trainer.*	*Warm-up* 200m easy freestyle and backstroke – 75m freestyle, 25m backstroke
200m freestyle – 75m Z2, 25m easy Z1	*Warm-up* 10 minutes Z1	100m freestyle – 25m hard, 25m easy
100m steady Z2 freestyle	4 x 1-minute hard efforts on a 1-minute Z2 recovery	*Main set* 10 x 400m freestyle on a 10-second RI as:
Main set 10 x 50m as: 25m drill-of-choice 1 into 25m freestyle	2 minutes Z2	4 x 400m Z2 3 x 400m Z3 2 x 400m Z4 1 x 400m Z5a
300m Z1 freestyle	*Main set* 4 x 12 minutes Z3 on an easy (5-minute) downhill recovery spin back to your starting point and repeat	*Cool down* 500m easy freestyle and backstroke – 75m freestyle, 25m backstroke
10 x 50m as: 25m drill-of-choice 2 into 25 freestyle	20 minutes Z2	**Bike – just-for-fun (PM)**
300m Z1 freestyle	*Cool down* 10 minutes easy Z1 spin	80 minutes easy
Cool down 200m Z1 freestyle	**Run – just-for-fun (PM)**	
	70 minutes easy	

Thursday	Friday	Saturday	Sunday
Bike (AM) – intensity set	**Swim – long/ strength**	**Long ride**	**Long run**
This set is best completed on the flat or a stationary bike trainer.	*Warm-up* 400m easy freestyle and backstroke – 75m freestyle, 25m backstroke	5 hours	180 minutes
Warm-up 10 minutes Z1		*Warm-up* 10 minutes Z1	*Warm-up* 10 minutes Z1
4 x 1-minute hard efforts on a 1-minute Z2 recovery	300m easy Z1 freestyle	10 minutes building to Z2	10 minutes building to Z2
2 minutes Z2	200m freestyle – 75m Z2, 25m easy Z1	60 minutes Z2	*Main set* 155 minutes Z2
Main set 2 x 20 minutes Z3 on an easy 3-4 minute spin	100m steady Z2 freestyle	*Main set* 1 x 15-minute 5 x 30-minute 1 x 15-minute efforts at IMRP on a 5-10 minute easy Z1/2 spin	Include walk breaks when necessary. A couple of minutes every 20-60 minutes is recommended.
Cool down 10 minutes easy Z1 spin	*Main set* 8 x 300m Z2 on a 10-second RI as:	*Cool down* 5 minutes easy Z1 spinning	*Cool down* 5 minutes easy Z1 running
Run – long interval set	1. Freestyle swim		
Warm-up 10 minutes Z1	2. Freestyle with paddles		
4 x 1-minute hard efforts (Z4)	3. Freestyle with paddles and pull buoy		
1 minute easy (Z2)	4. Freestyle with paddles, pull buoy and band		
2 minutes Z2	Repeat for a total of 2 sets.		
Main set 3 x 10 minutes Z4 on an easy 2-minute Z1 recovery jog	*Cool down* 500m easy freestyle and backstroke – 75m freestyle, 25m backstroke		
Cool down 10 minutes Z1			

Week 22:

3 Weeks
to race day

**REDUCED
WEEK**

Monday	Tuesday	Wednesday
Technique swim	**Brick (AM)**	**Swim – intensity set**
Warm-up 300m easy Z1 freestyle	*This set is best completed on a hill or, if a hill is unavailable, a stationary bike trainer.*	*Warm-up* 400m easy freestyle and backstroke – 75m freestyle, 25m backstroke
200m freestyle – 75m Z2, 25m easy Z1	*Warm-up* 10 minutes Z1	*Main set* 8 x 200m freestyle on a 20-second RI as:
100m steady Z2 freestyle	4 x 1-minute hard efforts on a 1-minute Z2 recovery	1. 25 hard, 175 easy
Main set 10 x 50m as: 25m drill-of-choice 1 into 25m freestyle	2 minutes Z2	2. 50m hard, 150m easy 3. 75m hard, 125m easy
300m Z1 freestyle	*Main set* 4 x 8 minutes Z3 on an easy (5-minute) downhill recovery spin back to your starting point and repeat	4. 100m hard, 100m easy 5. 100m hard, 100m easy 6. 75m hard, 125m easy
10 x 50m as: 25m drill-of-choice 2 into 25 freestyle	10 minutes Z2	7. 50m hard, 150m easy 8. 25m hard, 175m easy
300m Z1 freestyle	*Run off the bike* 10 minutes IMRP	*Cool down* 200m easy Z2 freestyle
Cool down 200m Z1 freestyle	*Cool down* 5-10 minutes Z1	
	Run – just-for-fun (PM) Easy 60-minute run	

Thursday	Friday	Saturday	Sunday
Bike (AM) – intensity set	**Swim – long/ strength**	**Long ride**	**Reduced long run**
This set is best completed on the flat or a stationary bike trainer.	*Warm-up* 400m easy freestyle and backstroke – 75m freestyle, 25m backstroke	3 hours	130 minutes
Warm-up 10 minutes Z1		*Warm-up* 10 minutes Z1	*Warm-up* 10 minutes Z1
	300m easy Z1 freestyle	10 minutes building to Z2	10 minutes building to Z2
4 x 1-minute hard efforts on a 1-minute Z2 recovery	200m freestyle – 75m Z2, 25m easy Z1	60 minutes Z2	*Main set* 115 minutes Z2
2 minutes Z2		*Main set* 1 x 15-minute 3 x 30-minute	
Main set 2 x 12-minutes Z3 on an easy 3-4 minute spin	100m steady Z2 freestyle	1 x 15- minute efforts at IMRP on a 5-10 minute easy Z1/2 spin	Include walk breaks when necessary. A couple of minutes every 20-60 minutes is recommended.
Cool down 10 minutes easy Z1 spin	*Main set* 8 x 250m Z2 on a 10-second RI as:		
	1. Freestyle swim	*Cool down* 5 minutes easy Z1 spinning	*Cool down* 5 minutes easy Z1 running
Run – long interval set	2. Freestyle with paddles		
	3. Freestyle with paddles and pull buoy	**Visualisation session**	
Warm-up 10 minutes Z1	4. Freestyle with paddles, pull buoy and band		
4 x 1-minute hard (Z4)			
1 minute easy (Z2)	Repeat for a total of 2 sets.		
2 minutes Z2	*Cool down* 500m easy freestyle and backstroke – 75m freestyle, 25m backstroke		
Main set 1 x 10 minutes Z3 on a 30-second easy Z1 recovery jog			
2 x 10 minutes Z4 on an easy 2-minute Z1 recovery jog			
Cool down 10 minutes Z1			

Week 23:

2 Weeks
to race day

**TAPER
2**

Monday	Tuesday	Wednesday
Day off or **Recovery bike/spin** 20-30 minutes Z1	**Bike fitness test** Refer to chapter 4	**Swim fitness test** Refer to Chapter 4

Thursday	Friday	Saturday	Sunday
Run fitness test	**Swim – long/ strength**	**Long ride**	**Reduced long run**
Refer to Chapter 4	*Warm-up*	2 hours	80 minutes
Visualisation session	400m easy freestyle and backstroke – 75m freestyle, 25m backstroke	*Warm-up* 10 minutes Z1	*Warm-up* 10 minutes Z1
	300m easy Z1 freestyle	10 minutes building to Z2	10 minutes building to Z2
	200m freestyle – 75m Z2, 25m easy Z1	30 minutes Z2	*Main set* 55 minutes Z2
	100m steady Z2 freestyle	*Main set* 2 x20-minute efforts at IMRP on 10-minute easy Z1/2 spin	*Cool down* 5 minutes easy Z1 running
	Main set 8 x 150m Z2 on a 10-second RI as:	*Cool down* 5 minutes easy Z1 spinning	
	1. Freestyle swim 2. Freestyle with paddles 3. Freestyle with paddles and pull buoy 4. Freestyle with paddles, pull buoy and band	**Visualisation session**	
	Repeat for a total of 2 sets.		
	Cool down 500m easy freestyle and backstroke – 75m freestyle, 25m backstroke		

Week 24:

Race Week

TAPER 1

	Monday	Tuesday	Wednesday	Thursday
	Easy 20 minute run to keep the legs moving. Or day off to pack the bike and ensure all is ready to go.	Travel followed by a short 20-minute walk or spin	**Run – intensity set** 40 minutes with short intensity segments *Warm-up* 10 minutes Z1 10 minutes Z2 *Main set* 2 x 4 minutes Z3 on a 1-minute easy Z1 recovery jog *Cool down* 10 minutes Z1 Massage if needed (recommended) but the massage must occur after the run	**Swim – intensity set** *Warm-up* 200m easy freestyle and backstroke – 75m freestyle, 25m backstroke 200m freestyle – 75m Z2, 25m easy Z1 100m steady Z2 freestyle *Main set* 5 x 100m as: 25 hard, 75 easy on a 10-second RI *Cool down* 500m easy freestyle and backstroke – 75m freestyle, 25m backstroke **Visualisation session**

Friday	Saturday	Sunday	Monday
Bike – intensity set	Day off if you can cope or very easy 20-minute run	Race Day Ironman Graduation	Party Day! Acceptance of your spot to Kona at the Roll Down Ceremony!
Warm-up 10 minutes Z1	Event check-in and race briefing	You have done the work, trust yourself, and believe in yourself and your ability. You will do great.	
10 minutes Z2	CHO loading		
Main set 2 x 4 minutes Z3 on a 1-minute easy Z1 recovery	**Optional visualisation session**	**Time to smash your Ironman**	
Cool down 10 minutes Z1			
Stretching			
Carbohydrate-rich meal for dinner			

SUBSTITUTE WEEKS FOR INCLUSION OF A HALF IRONMAN 70.3 IN THE BUILD UP

Week 12:

13 Weeks
to race day

**SUBSTITUTE
WEEK 12**

Monday	Tuesday	Wednesday
Swim – intensity set	**Brick (AM)**	**Run – tempo**
Warm-up 400m easy freestyle and backstroke – 75m freestyle, 25m backstroke	*This set is best completed on a hill or, if a hill is unavailable, a stationary bike trainer.*	*Warm-up* 10 minutes Z1 10 minutes Z2
Main set 8 x 200m freestyle on a 20-second RI as:	*Warm-up* 10 minutes Z1	*Main set* 2 x 8 minutes Z3 on an easy 5-minute Z2 recovery
1. 25 hard, 175 easy	4 x 1-minute hard efforts on a 1-minute Z2 recovery	*Cool down* 5 minutes Z1
2. 50m hard, 150m easy	2 minutes Z2	
3. 75m hard, 125m easy		
4. 100m hard, 100m easy	*Main set* 6 x 4 minutes Z3/4	
5. 100m hard, 100m easy		
6. 75m hard, 125m easy	All on an easy downhill recovery (2-3 minute downhill spin) back to your start position and repeat.	
7. 50m hard, 150m easy		
8. 25m hard, 175m easy		
Cool down 200m easy Z2 freestyle	*Run off the bike* 10 minutes Z3	
	Cool down 5-10 minutes Z1	

Thursday	Friday	Saturday	Sunday
Day off/ travel day	**Run**	**Bike**	**Race day 70.3 Half Ironman**
Recovery swim or just-for-fun bike	40 minutes with short intensity segments	*Warm-up* 10 minutes Z1	
Swim Easy 40-50 minute Z1 Freestyle	*Warm-up* 10 minutes Z1 10 minutes Z2	10 minutes Z2 *Main set* 2 x 4 minutes Z3 on a 1-minute easy Z1 recovery jog	
Or	*Main set* 2 x 4 minutes Z3 on a 1-minute easy Z1 recovery jog	*Cool down* 10 minutes Z1	
Bike Easy 50-60 minute Z1 Spin			
Visualisation session	*Cool down* 10 minutes Z1	**Visualisation session**	
	Carbohydrate-rich meal for dinner	CHO loading	
		Stretching	

Week 13:

12 Weeks
to race day

**SUBSTITUTE
WEEK 13**

	Monday	Tuesday	Wednesday
	Day Off	**Technique swim**	**Run – just-for-fun (PM)**
	Stretching	*Warm-up* 300m easy Z1 freestyle	60 minutes easy
		200m freestyle – 75m Z2, 25m easy Z1	
		100m steady Z2 freestyle	
		Main set 10 x 50m as: 25m drill-of-choice 1 into 25m freestyle	
		300m Z1 freestyle	
		10x50m as: 25m drill-of-choice 2 into 25 freestyle	
		300m Z1 freestyle	
		Cool down 200m Z1 freestyle	
		Bike – just-for-fun (PM)	
		60 minutes easy	

Thursday	Friday	Saturday	Sunday
Bike (AM) – intensity set	**Swim – long/ strength**	**Long ride**	**Long run**
		5hrs 30 mins	150 minutes
This set is best completed on a hill or, if a hill is unavailable, a stationary bike trainer.	*Warm-up* 400m easy freestyle and backstroke – 75m freestyle, 25m backstroke	*Warm-up* 10 minutes Z1	*Warm-up* 10 minutes Z1
		5 hrs 15 mins: target Z1/2	10 minutes building to Z2
Warm-up 10 minutes Z1	300m easy Z1 freestyle	Try to include a 2 x 30-minute Z3 effort.	*Main set* 105 minutes Z2
4 x 1-minute hard efforts on a 1-minute Z2 recovery	200m freestyle – 75m Z2, 25m easy Z1	*Cool down* 5 minutes easy Z1 spinning	Include walk breaks when necessary. A couple of minutes every 20-60 minutes is recommended.
2 minutes Z2	100m steady Z2 freestyle		
Main set 3 x 8 minutes Z3 on an easy 4-5 minute downhill spin	*Main set* 8 x 200m Z2 on a 10-second RI as:		*Cool Down* 5 minutes easy Z1 running
20 minutes Z2	1. Freestyle swim 2. Freestyle with paddles		
Cool down 10 minutes easy Z1 spin	3. Freestyle with paddles and pull buoy		
Run – tempo	4. Freestyle with paddles, pull buoy and band		
Warm-up 10 minutes Z1	Repeat for a total of 2 sets.		
10 minutes Z2	*Cool down* 500m easy freestyle and backstroke – 75m freestyle, 25m backstroke		
Main set 2 x 8 minutes Z3 on an easy 5-minute Z2 recovery			
Cool down 5 minutes Z1			

ACKNOWLEDGEMENTS

To all the great coaches, teachers and mentors I have had in all my endeavours. You have all taught me, inspired me and helped shape my views, allowing me to become the coach and educator that I am, and allowing me to achieve my impossible.

While there are too many to mention here, I would especially like to thank:

Bob Carter

Deb McMahon

Grant Giles

Joe Friel

Kevin Fergusson

Nigel Pietsch

Wendy Piltz

The Burnside Lacrosse Club

The Lakers Triathlon Club

The exceptional teachers at East Adelaide Primary School

The equally exceptional teachers at Concordia College

All the athletes I have ever been fortunate enough to coach and assist on their personal journeys.

As always, to Mum, Dad and Benjamin: let's just go with 'Thank you'.

A FINAL WORD

With your increased knowledge, you now have three options.

1. Follow this book and self-coach.

2. Find an Ironman coach to help you.

3. Disregard your new-found knowledge and do nothing!

But honestly, is that last point really an option? I want you to consider the investment that you're making in your Ironman triathlon, whether it's for one race or a series of races. What are you really putting into it? Time? Money? Effort? Emotion? Chances are you're investing all of these things in spades! It always amazes me how, despite making such a big investment, some people choose not to make a conscious effort to improve their training and racing. But naturally I would say that; I'm a coach and one of the converted.

Earlier in the book I planted a seed. A seed about how an Ironman coach can fast-track your improvement and provide an approach tailored to you as an individual. Hiring a coach helps you to improve your triathlon and Ironman knowledge. This helps to ensure that you get the best return on your investment (time, money, effort, emotion) based on your personal circumstances. The great thing about coaching is that it gives you structure and accountability, and when you have that, you don't have to think – you just need to do.

Warning: coaching and training plug coming up. (Hey, it's what I love.)

If you're looking for an Ironman triathlon coach, this is where The Kona Journey steps in. As the founder of The Kona Journey,

I believe everyone should be able to have fun training, completing Ironman races and qualifying for Kona. The Kona Journey's mission is to deliver inspirational and educational Ironman training programs leading to Ironman triathlete improvement, accomplishment and celebration. You have completed your best Ironman and qualified for Hawaii.

To help deliver this my team and I created The Kona Journey Membership. It is a Membership site that gives you access to Sprint, Olympic, Half and Full Ironman training programs and the relevant videos to take you from wherever you are now to being a better Ironman triathlete – one who achieves their impossible Ironman dream and gets to compete at the Ironman World Championships in Kona.

The training program takes you through the process of building up to your race outlined in this book. Over the years that I have coached other triathletes and trained and raced myself, the process (or journey, if you like) that people progress through has become clear. While everyone's journey is different and unique, there are similarities, such as consistent questions and concerns that come up at predictable times. I have taken all this knowledge and jam-packed it into The Kona Journey Membership.

Ultimately your journey will culminate with your Ironman graduation – your Ironman race – which (all going well) you will finish with a blaze of glory and qualification for Hawaii. This is where you will show off to your friends and family all the personal improvement that you have been working towards, and all that you have learnt on your journey. You will have developed your ability as a triathlete and your Ironman training knowledge – knowledge that will stay with you forever as you continue on your journey, reassess your goals and dream a bigger dream.

Some athletes will choose to self-coach, and there is absolutely no problem with this. If you choose this option, my hope is that the information in this book will help you to improve your Ironman triathlon training. I hope that you will be able to implement this new knowledge, along with your existing triathlon training knowledge, to follow a training plan that helps you reach your goals. From here I would encourage you to continue to find, implement and improve your triathlon knowledge as you continue on your great Ironman triathlon journey.

Finally, for those who are interested in 1v1 online triathlon coaching, we certainly offer this service and would love to have you on board as part of the team.

More information on The Kona Journey Membership and personal 1v1 online coaching can be found on The Kona Journey website: www.thekonajourney.net or by emailing info@thekonajourney.net

THANK YOU

As a little thank you for reading *Journey to Kona*, a tree has been planted on your behalf. I believe in giving back, as does the whole team at The Kona Journey, and we have decided to do it with trees. After all, as triathletes we're fond of the environment, and we suspect you are too. This way we will always have somewhere special to train, for you, for ourselves and for our children.

CPSIA information can be obtained
at www.ICGtesting.com
Printed in the USA
BVHW061404160222
629193BV00008B/117